A Piece of Danish Happiness

Sharmi Albrechtsen

A Piece of Danish Happiness

Sharmi Albrechtsen

ISBN 9781489565457

PRINTED IN THE UNITED STATES OF AMERICA

Cover Design by SharperDesign

First Paperback Edition

A Piece of Danish Happiness

Denmark has been ranked as the happiest nation in the world for the last 20 years.

In 1973, the European Commission set up a 'Eurobarometer' to find out about issues affecting its citizens. Since then member states have been surveyed about well-being and happiness.

Amazingly Denmark has topped the table every year since 1973.

This book was started to find the secret recipe for why the Danes were so happy.

Instead it is a story of my personal journey to understand the country that I live in and to find true happiness in my life in Denmark

Content

Happiness is like a cat

"Happiness is like a cat. If you try to coax it or call it, it will avoid you.

It will never come.

But if you pay no attention to it and go about your business, you'll find it rubbing against your legs and jumping into your lap."   *William J. Bennett*

After 10 years of living in Denmark, I have come to realize that Danes are cat lovers. Each year when the happiness data is revealed, they are pleasantly surprised. Then, they smile it off with a smug shrug and brush off the cat hair, "Hmm, yes I guess it is true. We are happy."

That said, when you ask them why, they are simply unable to provide an answer. They hedge around the answer, hem and haw and maybe point to their very fat social welfare program (universal health care, free schools, unemployment insurance, etc.) and attribute their happiness to that.

But hey, hang on a minute. Other countries across Europe have similar social welfare programs and they are not even close to the beating Denmark's lead position. I get the shrug and the smug Cheshire cat smile. Damn, I am allergic to bloody cats.

This is why I started a blog in 2010 on the official website for Denmark (www.Denmark.dk) it began as an online journal that would track my investigation into why Danes were so bloody happy interspersed with interviews, facts and my own personal journey to find Danish happiness. It eventually became a collaborative effort where thousands of Danes and people around the world would contribute.

You would think that living in the happiest country in the world would be pure, unbridled joy and bliss. In actuality, everyday life in Denmark is pretty harsh. After observing and living with the Danes, (married to two Danes and mother of a Danish child), I would have to counter that on the surface they don't actively seek happiness nor do they walk about looking particularly happy. On the contrary, many Danes on the street have a blank, zombie, stoned-faced look about them.

As a visitor, when you walk the streets of Copenhagen, do not expect to find a sea of smiling faces, whistling workers, friendly strangers or any type of the Disneyland-style of happiness behavior we Americans expect. This is not Thailand after all.

If you are ordering in a restaurant, your Danish waiter will probably be downright rude to you. 'Want another glass of Coke? You can go to the bar and order it yourself,' they will retort. In many Copenhagen cafes, the waiters do not take orders (only serve) and most do not receive or expect tips. Why would they? Plus, they earn around 25 dollars an hour. And by the way, your large Coke was 10 dollars.

A self-admitted shoe aficionado, I have been literally thrown out of a Copenhagen shoe shop. Was I causing a ruckus? Was I stealing shoes? No, the shoe shop would be closing in 15 minutes and I needed to be out the door.

'But someone was waiting on me. I just tried on a shoe,' I pleaded. 'Please leave, the shop is closing," I was told very sternly. (I am still in the shop as the security bars come down around the shop windows).

What happened to the rule, Customers Come First? Isn't the customer is always right, I thought to myself.

Apparently, not in this country. Customers are in the way.

- Move to a Danish neighborhood and expect your neighbors to invite you to their home?

  o Forget about it.

- Expect to have a friendly conversation with a Dane on the train or at the bus stop?

  o Don't think so.

- Need help with lifting a suitcase and expect that someone may offer help?

  o Not happening

- Expect that Danes would be interested in foreign visitors?

o   Nixen Bixen (no way in Danish), says my daughter.

Dear reader, do not confuse Danish contentment /happiness -subjective well-being with friendliness, good manners, polite behavior or any other such nonsense.

Danish happiness is hidden deep within.

And I was determined to find out its secret hiding place.

Where is Denmark You Ask?

When my Danish ex-husband (Mr. X) first told me he was from Denmark and asked me if I knew where it was located, I said 'It's somewhere in Sweden, right?'

On the Northern tip of Europe, Denmark is one of the smallest countries in the EU with just over 5.5 million people in its population.

Most people know it as the country that created the Danish – sweet flaky, buttery pastries filled with sweetened cream cheese, jam, chocolate or cream. In the Danish language, Danishes are called wienerbrød (Viennese bread) and they are simply scrumptious.

The Danes have lived in Denmark for over 200,000 years. In fact, it is one of the oldest kingdoms in the world. Denmark was once a very powerful nation, however, it has since been reduced in size to about one-third of its original territory.

The constant loss of territory and power and lack of any spectacular geographic landmarks might contribute to the now mild-tempered, humble nature of the Danes.

Many Danes say they have embraced their small, powerless country as part of their culture. Danes are happy that their country is small, manageable and has "hygge" (coziness) and think of their country as a peaceful, unremarkable perhaps slightly boring place.

Denmark is a tiny, unassuming country. Because of this, there are no grandiose dreams of becoming a Hollywood movie star, an NBA sports star or a millionaire. Only the Danish monarchy provides a bit of pomp and glamour in this small country.

The current Queen, Margrethe II, is regarded with affection and respect by the entire nation, and she and her family are featured in the media on a daily basis. Since becoming a royal is nearly impossible since it is a birthright and all the princesses and princes who have married into the royal family (are for some reason foreigners) – it is rare for a Danish commoner to become part of the royalty. So, little Danish girls don't even have the dream of becoming a princess.

With a few extravagant possibilities, Danes are modestly at peace with their lives. And for some reason, the happiest people in the world.

N - Europe

1. LITHUANIA
2. LUXEMBOURG
3. LIECHTENSTEIN
4. CZECH REPUBLIC
5. BOSNIA & HERZEGOVINA
6. SERBIA
7. MONTENEGRO
8. KOSOVO

Denmark and the World Happiness Data

Money can buy happiness, to a point

Denmark has consistently been in the top three in international surveys of happiness[i] for the last 20 years. This apparent satisfaction with life is often credited to 'soft factors' – culture, leisure time and family life - as opposed to 'hard values' such as money or material wealth.

That said, Denmark and the other Scandinavian countries all beat the U.S. in wealth as well with a GDP per capita according to the International Monetary Fund, the World Bank, and the CIA World Fact book. But this 'wealth' does not seem to be the leading factor in their happiness.

In the happiness research world, the Easterlin paradox -- also called the 'Frustrated Achievers paradox' is still considered groundbreaking. It was the first research to show that once your basic needs are met, more money does not increase your life satisfaction. Basically, money can only make a difference to your happiness if you are in a country where you are really struggling, ie. lacking proper housing, food and access to healthcare.

Easterlin writes that once basic needs are met, the average reported level of happiness does not change much with national income per person. For example, income per person rose steadily in the United States between 1946 and 1970 but the average person did not get much happier.

This is because materialistic aspirations, wants and dreams tend to increase proportionately to income over the life cycle and, therefore, the measurement of happiness decreases with material aspirations. As soon as you have more money, you increase expectations.

Even though most Americans are actively involved in the pursuit of happiness, the U.S. is still not even in the top 20 "happiest" nations according the World Database of Happiness[ii]. According to this source, the U.S.—one of the wealthiest countries in the world— ranks 23rd in overall life satisfaction, behind poorer countries like Costa Rica and Israel.

The surveys questioned people about their life satisfaction over a one-year time span. Were people satisfied? Did they feel as if their lives were filled by positive experiences and feelings, or negative ones? Did they have high expectations for the future?

In another study from a Gallup World Poll conducted in 140 countries. The poll asked respondents whether they had experienced six different forms of positive or negative feelings within the last day.

Some sample questions WERE: Did you enjoy something you did yesterday? Were you proud of something you did yesterday? Did you learn something yesterday? Were you treated with respect yesterday? In each country, a representative sample of no more than 1,000 people, age 15 or older, was surveyed. The poll was scored numerically on a scale of 1-100. The average score was 62.4.

Denmark earned the highest score, again, and was also shown to be highly productive. The United States' GDP earned an above-average score of 74, it did not break the top 10 in the happiness table. GDP per capita is often considered an indicator of a country's standard of living.

As we all know, money doesn't buy you love and it seems that wealth alone does not bring the greatest degree of happiness either. Norway had the highest GDP per capita on the list yet ranked ninth, not first in the studies.

A host of studies also point out that a happiness factor is work-life balance. While Scandinavian countries boast a high GDP per capita, the average work week is no more than 37.5 hours. This is really the case. Most of my colleagues and I work exactly 37 hours a week and the parking lot is empty at 4.30 p.m. Every day. Yet I must admit we are pretty damn productive.

In addition, there are studies that show Danish employees are some of the happiest and fulfilled workers in the world.

The conclusion of these studies was pretty obvious – a wealthy country does not necessarily equal happy and satisfied citizens. I needed to dig a bit deeper.

About Me (Om Mig)

My name is Sharmi and I will be your flight attendant on this tour to the happy country of Denmark.

Hmm... Are you American? You speak Danish with the 'cutest' accent!

Yes, that's me. The American girl, (with an Indian first name) living in Denmark who speaks Danish with the strongest accent this side of the Baltic Sea. I think my accent has grown stronger and more pronounced since I moved here, possibly as a subtle rebellion to forcibly learning Danish at the ripe old age of 27. It never really stuck. I guess being a Danish Language School drop-out didn't help either.

After more than 10 years in Denmark, I still speak with my broken *Danglish* and Danish people smile patiently at me with sometimes bewildered looks in their eyes. They should be mildly impressed that I try to speak a language that others have compared to 'talking with your mouth full of hot potatoes.'

I have stopped apologizing, turning a blind eye to my weakness, as I blame the left side of my brain, which I think closed off to new languages after my high school French teacher yelled at me for making fun of her teacher's pet for loving pâté. Ironically, I now make my daughter pâté (leverpostej) sandwiches on Danish rugbrød practically every day. It is the Danish version of the U.S. childhood favorite, peanut butter and jelly - except that it has no resemblance to a sticky, sweet PBJ. Leverpostej is ground pork livers, baked with lard and spread on a dense whole wheat brown bread.

Making my daughter's meals is a foray into culinary anthropology. Some of the things I make for her smell like cat food (meow!) and I would never, ever eat them myself in a million years. Intrigued by the mysterious smells and textures, like a good anthropologist I observe but do not participate. Oops, I digress.

Funnily enough, my poor spoken Danish has helped quite a bit when reflecting, researching and observing Danish society. In English, I am outspoken, gregarious and talkative – and never, ever lose an argument. Therefore, I don't listen very well.

But in Danish, I am polite, meek and smile a lot. I spend more time listening, observing and thinking rather than participating in discussions. Since my Danish comprehension is excellent, I can follow any conversation, even when some people are not expecting it ☺.

A Hindu American Princess (HAP) Not Born, But Created

I must admit that I had a challenging childhood. From the moment I set foot in my privileged elementary school, I was considered an FOB (Fresh off the Boat).

It was actually my immigrant parents who were fresh off the boat, since I was born in the U.S. They were the ones who spoke with heavy accents and wore funny, ill-fitting Indian clothes.

I remember my first days at my new elementary school in the posh suburb of Bethesda, Maryland. I was the only non-white child in my class. To make matters worse I had an unpronounceable name. Each morning during roll call, my teachers would butcher my name to the giggles of the class. Let me see, where is my chainsaw, this name is a difficult one, is that Shangri La? Shaaarm aaalaaaa?

Let me die. Please let me die right now. This harassment almost led to the permanent change in my name, to Sharmi. Even now, when people call me by my full name Sharmila, I get flashbacks to those endless tortuous grade school mornings.

Thanks to my Asian look and my parents' thick accents, on day one, I was automatically placed in the ESOL (English for Speakers of Other Languages) class even though I was fluent in English. ESOL (note the resemblance to ASSHOLE – it is pronounced the same way, too). Let's just say I felt much like Jack Nicholson's character in *One Flew Over the Cuckoo's Nest (trapped in a room, where people thought you couldn't speak your native tongue and forcing language lessons)* and was determined to get out of there ASAP.

To make matters even worse, my mother dressed me in the most heinous clothing possible. Red polyester pants, for example. Yes, it was the 70s but these were truly hideous even for those free-spirited days. During a sale, she bought like five pairs of the same pants in the same color. So other kids thought I smelled like curry (which I did) and I wore the same pants everyday- (which I did not).

Even in ballet class, I stuck out. My mother didn't buy me the standard pink leotard, white tights and perfect pink leather ballet slippers that all the little princesses had. Nooo, I got a blue yoga leotard she picked up at a garage sale, some nude nylon stockings with runs and a pair of black Chinese house slippers that squeaked when I tried to elegantly chassé across the room. I might as well have worn a t-shirt that said 'FOB loser' on it.

Of course, school lunches were also a problem. I carried a worn-out metal Wonder Woman lunch box but unlike the other kids with PBJ sandwiches, my mother tried to be 'innovative' by filling my thermos with chicken Vindaloo. When I complained about the smell, she tried to be 'multi-cultural' filling it instead with hot water and a warm wiener sausage. You can imagine my sheer humiliation each time, I pulled out a sausage from my thermos.

I was the odd one.

During my seemingly eternal elementary school days, my only friend was an Irish girl who was also 'banished' because she had hundreds of warts spread over her hands. I will never forget that sweet girl.

Unfortunately, her parents were divorced (to my parents' horror, I am currently on my third marriage) and my strict Indian parents disapproved of her family. This would be a recurring theme in my childhood – the bridging of my American upbringing and the social norms of an Indian family.

I am ashamed to say that I would have to hide her in the closet when she came to visit if my father happened to come home early from work. It didn't seem fair that the only person who would befriend me, the FOB Indian girl who had escaped ESOL, was unacceptable to my parents.

Things picked up when I starting working and earning my own money and began to create a world where my parents had no influence. My first job was at 13 and my first purchase was a pair of designer jeans. Those Gloria Vanderbilt jeans represented luxury and refinement for me. In those days, they cost 4 times a pair of jeans from Sears, yet I could clearly see the difference.

A huge golden signature on the back pocket of those jet dark blue jeans branded me as better and 'cool' and I realized I could 'buy' a new version of me. I loved wearing them, I instantly felt stunning and fashionable.

Unfortunately, the joy was short lived again when one of my classmates said to me:

'Do you only own one pair of jeans?'

'Errgh, not the plague of the red polyester pants again,' I grumbled.

I soon needed more of everything. I needed several pairs of designer jeans including Calvin Kleins, trendy leather docksider shoes to match, Ralph Lauren polo shirts in rainbow colors with the collars flipped up. Ok, it was the 80's.

These early experiences set the scene for the next 25 years of my life that I would spend scaling the social and materialistic ladder.

Fast forward to the end of my primary school days and to High School where I could be aptly described as a wannabe Hindu American Princess (HAP).

My high school, Walt Whitman, was the Washington, DC suburban version of the TV series "90210." The high school parking lot was full of luxury cars driven by a mix of affluent Washingtonians and international students whose diplomat parents worked at the World Bank, various international embassies and the International Monetary Fund.

While I was surrounded by wealth – the other students lived in huge McMansions and belonged to Country Clubs. My Indian family and I lived in a modest 60s split level home and were members of the local YMCA. We were comfortable. My father was a local statesman, politician and psychologist. My mother was an Indian American socialite.

On the surface, I had a good life that many teens would have been happy with: a vintage Mercedes at 16, close friends and stylish clothes. I was a member of the rich, international and cool Eurotrash clique.

But on the inside, I was a wreck and extremely discontented. The prosperity around me made me feel inadequate and I was always trying to make up for what I didn't have. I had high levels of stress trying to keep up with the proverbial Joneses, my classmates.

An age-old but revealing study shows that most people would rather live in a world in which they receive an annual salary of $50,000, when others are earning $25,000, than to earn an annual salary of $100,000 when others are making $200,000. This study resonates with me. While my family was comfortable, it was terrible for me to be the 'relatively' poor girl in an ocean of affluent friends and classmates.

I was ashamed to host them in my home which was much smaller, smelling of curry spices and badly furnished with a bric-a-brac of old furniture and la-z-boys, heavy lace curtains and tacky Indian artwork. Most of my teenage memories were spent out and about, nowhere near my childhood home.

I was working two jobs while studying full-time in order to pay for my shopping and keep up my image. As I built my wardrobe, I made sure that it had a classic timeless luxurious style. Needless to say, I never ever wore ethnic clothes even when they were considered hip.

I will never forget the blow-out argument I had with my very practical Sears and Kmart mother about the Guy Laroche designer prom dress priced at 750 USD (today's price 2000 USD) that I forced her to buy me at Bloomingdale's. The next day, I came home to find out that she had second thoughts and returned the dress to the store. I was so devastated, I ran away from home, walking the streets for hours, crying. I'll never forget that day. It was when I realized no one really understood me and the pressures I had.

How could my mother have done this to me? Sometimes I wondered if I could have been switched at birth...where were my real parents? I was sure that they were golfing at the Kenwood Country Club wondering where their long-lost daughter could be? This feeling of not belonging to my family would stay with me for the rest of my life.

Here's a story of what started a lifelong obsession: my first Gucci handbag that I scraped all my money together and bought. (I carried it proudly in high school even though technically it was a cosmetics pouch.)

But I soon found, as I would with many material things to come, that the initial excitement and joy was short-lived, almost fleeting. After a few months, I already had my eye on the next conquest, another Gucci handbag and after that, another and another.

Years later at the tender age of 25, I was newly divorced (after a quick but unsuccessful marriage to a well-to-do investment banker), living beyond my means and was slowly drowning in credit card bills, unpaid student loans and car payments.

My obsession with materialism followed me for years. It was not until I moved to Denmark in 1997, that I would try to give up all my credit cards and <u>attempt</u> to follow a less materialistic life.

I would find that this was not an easy feat. Old habits die hard.

It is not the level of prosperity that makes for happiness but the kinship of heart to heart and the way we look at the world. Both attributes are within our power, so that a man is happy so long as he chooses to be happy, and no one can stop him.

Insights into the Mind of a Shoe Shopping Addict (Me)

It takes an addict to truly explain addiction. Like many women, I am into shoes. Big time. There is something so lovely about not ever having to worry about changing your size, at least your shoe size.

Unlike other areas of the body that change with seasons, such as the after holidays bloat, your shoes will always fit and look great. As one of my male friends once said to me, shoes are like tires for the feet. You would never buy cheap tires, so why would one buy cheap shoes?

Before I began my investigation into Danish happiness and cut back on my shoe collection, I probably owned more than 200+ pairs of shoes – most costing at least 400 USD each.

I had a special closet just for my shoes, they were lined up like colorful lollypops, each shining pair perfect – just waiting to be taken out to impress with a coordinated dress.

One of my role models is the mythical Carrie Bradshaw of "Sex and the City" fame. Carrie was a lover of gorgeous, luxurious shoes and clothes. She is the much loved darling of millions of women who identified with her emotional attachment to shoes. Carrie was someone who regularly maxed out her credit cards to buy new Jimmy Choo's and Manolo Blahniks.

She made it ok, even stylish, for women to come out of their shoe closets and admit their addiction. And just as many were inspired to follow Carrie's financially disastrous but incredibly indulgent lead.

In the TV series, Carrie "lived for fashion," and confessed to choosing to buy *Vogue* magazine instead of food. A notorious shoe lover with a insatiable hunger for expensive designer shoes (notably Manolo Blahniks, but also Christian Louboutin and Jimmy Choo), Carrie claimed she had spent over $40,000 on shoes.

Carrie's amazing shoe collection appeared to be excessive on a newspaper journalist's salary. Indeed, her girlfriends on the show often commented that they were surprised she could afford her shopping addiction.

Carrie much like me occasionally maxed out credit cards. She couldn't buy her condo because of her non-existent savings and a bad credit rating thanks to her extensive shopping. She once joked that she might "literally be the woman who lived in her shoe."

Like for many young women, Carrie was someone for me to aspire to. She was the ultimate chic, fashionable woman living a fantastic and glamorous life.

The hypocrisy of a similarly shoe-obsessed woman, Imelda Marcos with her 2,700 pairs of shoes, did not warrant the same kind of appreciation or envy. Imelda was ridiculed and harassed for her excessiveness. The irony was that, unlike Carrie, Imelda was born wealthy and privileged and could actually afford these luxuries.

The Danes on the other hand, had a culture of practical, comfortable shoes. ECCO, Dansko and Børn are international companies that produce and 'market' the sensible Danish shoe. Ugly, clunky and definitely rubber heeled, these reasonably priced clog type shoes were ubiquitous.

Much like in the pioneer days, Danish women walked and biked everywhere and their shoes endured wind, rain, snow as well as mud paths and the dreaded cobblestone paths. These paths, while I concede are old-world and charming, are a death to any beautiful heeled shoe.

I had more than a few accidents where my precious stilettos were destroyed by being jammed between two cobblestones. Thanks to inertia, these accidents caused me to trip, fly forward and land on my knees in a 'praying to Allah' position. Thanks to the Jante law, most people just walked by snickering sardonically that it serves me right wearing such impractical high heels instead of the practical clogs that most Danish women wore.

I couldn't bear the thought of wearing comfortable shoes, OK perhaps some sneakers at the gym, even though I would have enjoyed the freedom of walking without pain. I admitted, there were definitely times I regretted wearing impractical shoes, as I hobbled down the rain and sleet stained sidewalks of Copenhagen, praying that I would not trip and fall.

After a city walk together, my friend Charlotte's husband, Lars, gave me a forced mini lecture on how few shoes he owned and how it really had no meaning whatsoever for his image. He said that all shoes were a functional clothing item and a shoe sole did not embody the soul of the wearer. He talked and talked, blabbity, blah, I stared at his ECCO hydrid street sneaker.

I was so annoyed, I decided that I would prove him wrong and found this one-off piece of research on different types of shoes and whether people felt that they symbolized the wearer's personality.

In the study, published in the Journal of Research in Personality, the researchers polled undergraduate students to look at photos of favorite shoes that were provided by fellow students. The students were asked to rate the wearers' personae, for example, whether they were clingy or detached in their relationships, etc.

The shoe owners were asked to describe their attitudes and behavior. Researchers found that there was a significant correlations between several personality traits and relationship styles – and shoe types! Ahaha! I triumphantly said to myself.

For example, the study cites that students rated those persons wearing high top sneakers and masculine shoes as having less agreeable personalities, which matched with the self-assessments. They also said that people who wore neutral shoe colors (brown, tan, gray, black) were more likely to have anxiety over their relationships. But those who wore more colorful shoes had more confidence in their relationships.

Some of the conclusions drawn, however, were fairly obvious: Nice-looking and fashionable shoes were correctly correlated with a higher income. Weirdly enough, *in this study* men tended to wear more expensive shoes than women.

For my part, I had to ask was the excess of my shoes a way of buying acceptance, appreciation and admiration? What was the image I was giving – chic and elegant or frivolous and overindulgent? Regardless,

I wasn't getting any such response from the Danes, most seemed to ignore my shoes. But even without their approval or admiration, I did feel some kind of high when I bought a stunning pair of shoes.

I had always been fascinated by the work of Danish marketing guru, Martin Lindstrom who studied the effects of colors and fragrances on people. Lindstrom and his team of neuroscientists used MRI technology to observe the power our senses have on what we buy.

He found that 90 percent of the women in his study increased their heart rate when they saw the quintessential robin-egg blue Tiffany boxes. Other persons examined felt an increased pulse when they inhaled a new car scent.

I experienced all of those bodily effects when I opened a box with a new pair of unworn designer shoes. The crackling of the tissue paper, the smell of fine Italian leather, digging into the bottom of the box to find the velvet soft shoe bags and authenticity cards gave me pure pleasure.

They represented luxury, excitement and total newness. They stayed deliciously fresh until the first time I wore them and then, each time after, the joy I experienced with them slowly faded and they were moved to the back of my shoe closet waving goodbye to me as I purchased new 'friends' to replace them.

Falling In Love in London, Moving to Denmark

I left the U.S. with a bankruptcy pending, a spree of unpaid credit cards and only 900 USD in my pocket. Until I received my first paycheck in London, I was on a shoestring budget and sneaking food from my roommate's side of the refrigerator.

I moved to London to be with one of the great loves of my life and my daughter Nina's dad, now called the X. He was a hot shot Danish lawyer living in London and represented finesse, sophistication plus he had a drop dead gorgeous foreign accent and a dazzling smile.

I loved it in London. The X introduced me to extraordinary bars and restaurants – a real jet-set life. I thought I had died and gone to heaven. He was amazing and drove a really cool 5-series BMW. He had a company condo overlooking the Thames River and the Tower Bridge and great taste. We had a refined and sophisticated life together.

During the week, we worked at our jobs in London, and on the weekends we would often take a weekend in the English countryside, staying in one of the many mansion estate cum hotels that served gourmet breakfasts on fine bone porcelain and sterling silver cutlery.

The HAP in me loved the shops, London had all the major brands – Burberry, Louis Vuitton, Gucci - and I shopped there with glee and gusto. After I moved in with X and we married, I had no living expenses and could spend all my extra income on clothes, handbags and shoes.

I had a distant and faded vision we would eventually move to Denmark. We had experienced a couple of nice but VERY short holidays in Copenhagen – I had been to the Tivoli Gardens and had lunch in Nyhavn. I felt ready to take on the Danes and move to Denmark. And then it happened right after the wedding. It was time to move and I started packing for my new adventure.

While it was only an hour's flight from London, Copenhagen was another world. And so the next chapter of my life began. I had read a little about Denmark before I moved but I wasn't prepared for the major culture shock I experienced moving from cosmopolitan London to little Copenhagen.

Taxes, wages, restaurants, food, cars – everything was crazy expensive. If I thought that moving to London was reducing the value of my dollar, moving to

Denmark seemed like the dollar was no better than Monopoly play money. Gas prices were up to 10 USD a gallon.

But X smoothed my way, I was his new American wife and he wanted me to feel comfortable and relaxed in his country. I will never forget my first uber expensive designer Gucci briefcase the X had bought for me to celebrate my first job in Denmark. My heart skipped a beat when we bought it together and I still have it. It was an elegant, charcoal grey monogrammed briefcase with soft leather handles. Just being in that shop where it was purchased made me feel special. I will never forget the rush and the pride I had in receiving such a luxury item. It made me feel confident and fashionable.

And the briefcase was another reminder that luxury items would continue to play an important role in my identity as a woman – desperately wanting to be fashionable and chic, wanting to be like Carrie Bradshaw

Life In Denmark

Luckily, I was able to move my job from London to Copenhagen and I rented an office in a small office hotel on Strøget (the pedestrian shopping area in Copenhagen). This was the beginning of my remote, isolation days. Suddenly, the X was back in the HQ office of his law firm on track for making partner which meant that I was soon abandoned as he worked more than 70 hours a week.

My boredom would soon be cured by my new friends: Gucci, Louis and Prada who all awaited me with open doors and branded shopping bags down on the Strøget. X was always home late and unable to tell me exactly when he would be home. We stopped having dinner together. And when he finally did come home, he would need to 'relax and rewind' from his day by watching TV or playing video games. Many nights, he would fall asleep on the sofa.

Often we had fights about my excessive spending and his terribly long working hours. Ironically, when he made partner (and started working 85 hours a week), we stopped fighting about both since soon we had plenty of money despite the tough Danish tax system. I started to ignore his working hours and found other hobbies to keep me busy -- like shopping.

We had a small but lovely home, I gave birth to a sweet baby girl and I had a great career as a communications manager. Yet something was missing for me. Five years after moving to Denmark, I was no longer contributing to our household with my income, although I was working full-time. I kept my promise of no more credit card debt. Instead all the money I earned, nearly 5000 USD after tax per month was spent on buying stuff.

As those of you shoppers/fashionistas out there know, 5K does not get you very far at Louis Vuitton. A handbag, a couple of pairs of shoes and you are done! At the time I rationalized since X was working so hard, I could at least enjoy the financial side effects.

Unfortunately, I did not stop with just spending all of my income on clothes, bags and shoes. I also set my sights on a new car to match my newly groomed look. After tears and numerous heated fights with the X, I got my BMW convertible, 3-series. In DK, cars have a 180 percent tax so being interested in cars is not a good habit. But I got what I wanted. It was amazing, fast and beautiful. As a young woman, driving a pretty fancy sports car, I felt satisfied that I had finally made it.

In hindsight, I can't believe I could not see the pattern and I am embarrassed now to write this or even admit that I was so obsessed with status. During these years of my spending, I lived in a self-created ex-patriot womb. Most of my friends were foreigners who were in Denmark on special assignments. Whilst my friends and I had tried briefly to make friends with the local Danes, most of us found it fruitless and decided to hang out with each other instead.

Making friends with Danes was tough because most of them kept to themselves and seemed very, very tired with their simple and seemingly boring lives. From an outsiders view, it seemed like they did not really have room for more friends in their lives – nor did they seem to do anything fun like shop or go to expensive restaurants. For example, my in-laws had less than a handful of friends and most of their entertaining was with extended family. Plus, since my Danish was pretty unintelligible, any potential Danish friend needed to be fluent in English to keep up with me and think that it was worthwhile to keep up the friendship. Too much hassle...I think.

Anyhow, I didn't need them I told myself and put it out of my mind.

As Will Rogers says, too many people spend money they haven't earned, to buy things they don't want, to impress people they don't like. That was me.

Although I had always been a spender, life in Denmark seemed to be making it much worse. One of my other problems was that Danes were not impressed with my materialistic stuff. I think in the past, especially in the U.S. and London, whenever I flashed my newest luxury fashion items around I received admiration and encouraging comments. People noticed me and there are always remarks and compliments given by friends, colleagues and even strangers.

Here in Denmark, I received nothing. The reserved nature of the Danes and their opinions about 'show' meant that any materialistic show-off behavior of mine was met with contempt. Or worse disinterest. It was like people didn't seem to care what I was wearing or carrying. No one ever noticed, nor did they care or recognize what the brands were.

I will never forget the conversation I *tried* to have with some mothers at the ice skating rink while I was impatiently waiting for Nina to get off the damn ice. Finally the mundane conversation steered away from the new kind of muesli cereal that was available in the Irma grocery store, to shoes! 'Hey, a subject I know,' I said under my breath as I quickly woke up from my comatose state.

The conversation went something like this:

'I like your shoes. They are really adorable,' said Danish skating number one to Danish skating mom number 2, pointing to a pretty scary looking comfortable shoe flat bootie with laces.

'Thanks, they are really comfortable and they look good, too' said Danish skating mom 2

I was speechless for a moment, feeling like I was from another planet but hey, at least the conversation was shoe related. 'Yes, they do look really comfortable. But I feel for work I need something with a heel,' pointing to my new discreet heather grey leather and patent Chanel pumps with a peep toe.

And then, they paused and said nothing. They just looked at me and smiled, pretended I did not exist and continued to talk to each other about other *comfort shoes*.

'How bloody rude,' I thought to myself. 'I did try to make an effort. Just because I don't wear repulsive comfort shoes, doesn't mean I should be excluded.'

Of course, there is a small population of Danish women who shop for designer clothing and fashion items but they are few and far between. And they most certainly did not have the obsession that I did about it.

On the other hand, I did discover that Danish design impressed people. It was something that Danes recognized and coveted. In Denmark, since restaurants are so prohibitively pricey, there is a lot more home dining that in other countries. So if I couldn't impress people with my shoes, handbags and BMW convertible – a Danish mansion house filled with designer furniture could be the answer, I thought.

There is a backstory that illustrates my twisted psyche with regards to homes. Below is an example of my fixation with dream homes even at the tender age of 10.

As earlier established, I had an unfulfilling, mediocre childhood and pretty much any dream or desire that I ever had when I was child never came to fruition. My parents never went out of their way to make me happy, it wasn't part of their 'job', they said. One of my distinct childhood dreams was to own a *Barbie Dreamhouse*, (a huge dollhouse for Barbie dolls). My only friend (the girl with the warts) got one for Christmas (fully furnished), it was soo huge that in order to properly play with it, her mother was forced to store it in their living room.

Barbie's Dreamhouse was the coolest California beach mansion house with modern lemon yellow walls. It could break up into three different parts. It also had big white French doors, flower boxes and terracotta roof. Barbie had a groovy green & pink velvet Panton inspired sofa and chair set and a Le Corbisier style extra large vanity makeup table, where she could gaze at herself while applying blue eye shadow and brushing her long, perfect straight blonde hair.

I remember asking my parents for this Barbie dream house (every birthday and Christmas for four years) but knowing deep in my heart that it would never, ever happen. My mother was a practical soul and spending 30 dollars on a child's toy was out of the question. Instead, my sister and I made our own Barbie 'ghetto' apartment building out of cardboard boxes with furniture fashioned out of milk cartons and empty toilet rolls. My grandmother bought me a $3.99 inflatable latex couch and chair set from Woolworth's that was made for knock off Barbie dolls called Polly. Boy, we had class.

Fast forward 30 years later and thanks to the blessing of E-bay, I actually bought an original, vintage 70's Barbie dreamhouse with coordinating designer furniture with the excuse that I would give it to my daughter for her birthday. The shipping charges alone cost me 300 USD – it was quite the generous gift.

Quite honestly, Nina precociously rejected it, since she was the avid professional collector of every new Barbie and accessory on the market (thanks to me) and could not understand why she should have a warn-out, cracked and dusty plastic dollhouse instead of the latest, glossy bright pink Barbie townhouse that her friends had.

'I don't want this,' she said firmly. My heart broke in tiny pieces and I could not help showing my disappointment. 'None of my friends have a dollhouse this ugly. It's not even Barbie style – why is it yellow?'

'What,' I said in disbelief. 'Can't you see how wonderful it is?', as I sat Barbie crookedly down on one of the unstable retro kitchen chairs. I even offered to help her play with it and maybe buy some new pink Barbie furniture to make it her own.

While I encouraged her to embrace the house, hoping she could find the joy that I had dreamt about as a child. I had a sinking feeling that I screwed up again 'buying something that I wanted instead of thinking of the person I was giving to.'

Alas, the vintage Barbie dream house ended in the garbage (like many of my dreams) after the divorce.

Although X and I owned a small 1930's home in one of the best neighborhoods outside of Copenhagen, my new obsession became a mega-dream house with all the Danish design trimmings. The X did not have the same needs or dream and he was very reluctant. He was content in our house and he kept trying to change my mind by changing the subject or putting off the 'talk'.

But I would not give up. All of these pent up desires from childhood and life were fueling me. I wanted worldly enjoyment, the pleasure of living in magnificence and the exquisiteness of every material pleasure that money could buy.

I had a massive gaping hole inside me and I just knew that if I had my dream house, the right house, I would finally be at peace and be happy. I felt I deserved it, too. I was basically alone – I left my family, friends and country to be here and well, X should tap into his gigantic bank account and buy me (oh, I meant us) a dream home.

For the psychologist Carl Jung, a house was a near reincarnation of one's self. Jung actually described his home/building project on Lake Zurich. Jung spent more than thirty years building this castle-like home, and he believed that the towers and annexes represented his psyche.

Clare Cooper Marcus, a Professor of Architecture at the University of California in Berkeley, has written extensively about the relationship between homes and the people who live in them. Her book *House as a Mirror of Self* explores the meaning of "Home" as a place of self-expression, as a place of nurturance, and as a place of sociability.

These examples are not unusual and I was not alone in this real estate fanaticism. An American news poll in 2012 found that almost 90 percent of Americans believe that homeownership is an important part of the American dream.

No-one better than me realized the power of nagging and persistence as I struggled to make this dream home come to fruition. Every few months, I would casually call a real estate agent to come round and give an estimate on our small house. Armed with the estimate, I would appeal to X with a reassuring 'look how much money' we can make speech.

Nearly three years after my first idea of selling our first home and buying the Sharmi Dream House, he finally relented.

Here's how it unfolded

I had just received an inflated 11 million Danish Kroner estimate from a real estate agent (we had bought the house for less than 3 million, eight years earlier). I pulled out the estimate and placed it in the middle of the dining room table. I knew that X was getting tired of my antics but I was all the more determined to show him that *now* was the time.

'What's for dinner?', said X, plopping into a kitchen chair, munching a carrot stick and pushing away the estimate.

Dinner, but hey, what the.... 'Look, I said, now taking out the big guns and flashing the Divorce card. 'I want to talk about our future together.'

'Okaaay,' said X with a worried tone.

'Couples need to have dreams together and build a life together,' I moaned. 'Moving is really important for me. I need a change, I need this and we need this.'

'Alright, alright. Let's take a look at some Open Houses, this weekend.' he said.

Little did I know that my house obsession would start our marriage on an emotional rollercoaster ride that was combined with a nightmarish spooky funhouse.

We were indulgent and bought the 6000 square foot mega dream house first. On one of the most expensive streets in Copenhagen, the street Viggo Rothesvej was a grandeur playground for the wealthy and famous.

The posh road is named after a politician and railroad entrepreneur, Viggo Rothe, who expanded the Copenhagen rail system so that trains covered the rest of Zealand and through to Jutland. He actually never lived in Charlottenlund, preferring a modest home in Copenhagen overlooking the central railroad station.

Graceful mansions lined the streets, each one delightful and magnificent with imposing lawns and all shadowed beneath the Danish botanical gardens filled with 10 meter high gorgeous oak and birch trees, scented tea roses and musky pine bushes. Most homes had backyards with their own private entrance into the gardens.

It was a gorgeous Italian style rambling mansion with cathedral windows, an impressive hall graced with wide mahogany staircase, high French oak paneled ceilings, recessed mahogany bookcases, and beautiful hardwood floors.

I never forgot walking into the formal dining room – it was like a banquet room – a mini Versailles with floor to ceiling French doors and the most dazzling and stunning ceiling with intricate deep crown molding and a massive center medallion.

Again, I had visions of being the hostess of swanky parties with a martini in one hand, casually gliding around the house and showing off our amazing home to our friends and family. When my American family came to visit, they would have their own wing of the house with a private bath and even a tea kitchen.

Moving up the Downton Abbey style staircase, the master bedroom had its own sitting area with glass double French doors into the high ceilinged bedroom, where I imagined myself drinking sweet tea and relaxing with a book on a light blue, silk embroidered settee.

David Soul once said. 'Yes, your home is your castle, but it is also your identity and your possibility to be open to others.' This was my mantra, the house was my dream, it was my image, identity and it became a symbol of my marriage or at least a beautiful mirage for what my marriage should have been.

The market was up and we were confident our home would sell fast. So we started renovating our new home to be fitted with designer Italian bathrooms and hand-built custom kitchens. Our plan was to finish the expensive renovations and then we would sell our current home and move in to our McMansion. These were some of the happiest days of my marriage to X – we actually shopped together! Buying up designer Arne Jacobsen chairs for our new home, the shiny built-in Nespresso café latte machine, Phillip Starck bathtubs and basically creating a new designer life together was a dream.

This mega home would symbolize my 'arrival' into upper class society with status, glamour and wealth, I told myself. I believed I would finally be able to be 'rid' of my FOB middle class past.

During our six months shopping and renovation 'trip,' we didn't see the dark cloud that was emerging. Around that time the housing market bubble burst, the financial crisis was officially announced and buyers for our 'old' home were suddenly scarce.

One of our last dinners together was in our neighborhood Italian bistro, when he made the comment: 'Sharmi, you are the type of person who always chooses from the back of the wine list.'

What he was trying to say was: 'Sharmi, you are a fake who just buys the expensive stuff to appear classy instead of making intelligent decisions based on taste.'

Those days were probably the worst I have ever experienced. I felt scared, sick and powerless. No one wanted our 'old' home for eight months, as the market continued to spiral downward. The X started to slowly fall into a severe depression blaming me for everything. Yes, maybe we had agreed to buy the new house together but we both knew that it was my materialistic vision that had gotten us into this nightmare and possibly would take us to the brink of bankruptcy.

Although we eventually sold our home at a significant loss, my marriage never recovered. The day we turned over the keys to the new owner was also the day that we split up for good ......changing my life forever and finally forcing me to break my materialistic patterns for good.

My Wake-Up Call

It is often said that we fail to achieve happiness if we search for it. It's an unexpected side effect.

Philosophers have been searching for the answer to this question for hundreds of years. Aristotle started the debate, with his question about happiness and the practice of virtue.

One of Aristotle's most influential works is the Nicomachean Ethics, where he presents a theory of happiness that is still relevant today, more than 2300 years later.

Aristotle stated that happiness (also being well and doing well) is the only thing that humans desire for its own sake, unlike riches, honor, health or friendship. He said that people sought riches, or honor, or health not only for their own sake but also in order to be happy.

Happy people are virtuous, meaning they have outstanding abilities and emotional tendencies which allow them to fulfill our common human ends. For Aristotle, happiness is "the virtuous activity of the soul in accordance with reason." In short, happiness is the practice of virtue.

Was I living with virtue? A morally excellent or virtuous person has a character made up of virtues valued as good. She is honest, respectful, courageous, forgiving, and kind, for example. Because of these virtues or positive character traits, she is committed to doing the right thing no matter what the personal cost, and does not bend to impulses, urges or desires, but acts according to values and principles.

On reflection, my destructive and materialistic ways, were hurting me and my 7-year old daughter. I was just 38 years old and yet had two divorces behind me. I did not want to be known and remembered as a money-oriented, indulgent and greedy person.

In addition, as a newly minted divorcee I was faced with paying exorbitant rent for an apartment, food, internet, heat and insurances on my salary alone. My new reality was knocking on my door and I was worried that my new circumstances would cause me to tumble into despair and into welfare. Even though I had recently had a salary raise, only one-third of it ended in my bank account – the rest was eaten away by Danish taxes.

Although, I had a pretty civil Danish divorce and I received a divide from our combined assets we had together. But I was really scared. I was a divorced mom in a foreign country where I had few friends, no family and did not speak the language very well.

I must admit that my first panicky thoughts were run to the airport and fly home. Yes, I would move back to the States, a place where people understood me. A country where I belonged and I would rebuild myself – maybe marry another wealthy guy and get myself back on track.

But reality hit me like a ton of bricks, of course. I was no longer just 'ME', anymore I now had shared custody of my daughter. My sweet, little, perfect daughter who looked at me with her big brown eyes and called me 'Mor' in Danish. She belonged in Denmark where her father, cousins and grandparents were.

Born in Denmark, she was a Dane through and through. Her father, one of the top lawyers in Denmark made sure that we signed a non negotiable custody agreement and that it would be illegal for me to move her.

I could take many things – humiliation, exclusion, loneliness but even if I lost everything, one thing, I would not lose was my daughter. I swallowed the bitter pill and made the decision that, yes, I would be staying in Denmark.

Funnily enough, I came to Denmark for romantic love and I stayed in Denmark for the love of my daughter and remain in Denmark for the love of myself.

The Danish philosopher, Søren Kirkegård also gave me something to think about in his writings. He believed that as a physical being, man is always turned toward the outside, thinking that his happiness lies outside of himself. But when he finally turns inward, he discovers that the source of his happiness is within him.

After my second divorce, it became very apparent to me that I needed a change in perspective and to start looking inward. For years, I had assumed that my role on Earth was to worship the goddess of wealth. I believed that wealth symbolized success and would lead me to happiness. Instead I found the opposite to be true.

One of the few Danish friends I had at the time, commented: "You are NOT - the car you drive, the house you live in and the shoes you wear."

I began to realize that no matter how much I identified with my possessions, my Gucci bags would never love me back!

It was then that I started my quest. It seemed that the answer was right in front of me, yet it actually took Oprah Winfrey's visit to Denmark in 2009 to give me the real wake-up call.

When the Danish happiness data was released again in 2009, Oprah came to Copenhagen to produce a show about Danish happiness and that started me thinking. Is it really true? Is free healthcare, free education, and all the jazz that comes with social welfare the true key to happiness?

Oprah's quest was to find out why the Danes are so happy. She visited several families and concluded that Danes were the happiest people around because they didn't have to worry about healthcare or sending their children to college because 'everything's paid for.'

But I questioned just how happy Danes can be when taxes are so high in order to pay for the 'free' education and healthcare. In addition, the latest happiness survey pointed out that other Scandinavian and European countries with 'free' education and health care did not even rank inside the happiness top ten.

Indeed, poorer countries such as Bhutan and the Bahamas which have large differences in wealth distribution are among the top 10 happiest nations. In developed countries, reported levels of happiness do not increase with income. So a paradox existed.

This data led to great debates with my Danish and foreign friends and colleagues.

One American expat friend was incredulous.

"Happiest in the world- what a scam! Has anyone come to Denmark and walked around – no one is laughing, no one is smiling and the sales people here are the rudest I have ever experienced? They can't be serious," she concluded.

Yes, I admitted, "Danes were pretty strange. People do not wear their happiness on the sleeves or even on their faces. In fact, most people seem kinda grumpy....'

None of it made sense to me. When I looked into it, all of the data seemed to focus on income and wider economic and social political environments as the reasons for happiness.

And yes, it is true that wealthier countries are happier. But there are many wealthy countries including the U.S. that are not even in the top ten. Why are the Danes so happy?

Perhaps ideology, feelings, beliefs, and desires are the true key to happiness. But what was so special in Denmark? I had to wonder.

Before I dropped out of my Danish classes, the instructors told us about the Janteloven (the Jante law). It is a Danish mindset which devalues individual efforts and personal achievement and places all importance on the collective. Most considered this to be a terrible thing – it seemed un-American to me and against the concept of individual success and therefore happiness.

I had to admit that maybe the Jante law explained why Danes lead the world in the happiness rankings and have a unique mechanism for managing expectations and 'keeping it real.'

These cultural norms may help Danes focus on other attributes in life such as community, family, leisure time, environment and free choices instead of consumerism and material goods.

My first step was to investigate the data and dig into the thing we call happiness. I was sure that the answers were with the experts.

The Impossible American Dream

"The owners of this country know the truth: It's called the American dream because you have to be asleep to believe it." George Carlin

The thing is, I don't think I was different from most Americans who dreamt the American Dream. In the U.S., it is perfectly fine and acceptable to hunger for prosperity and success as well as fantasize about upward mobility.

Tons of infomercials on television promised ways to become a millionaire and there are hundreds of books promising riches and fame – One Minute Millionaire, Think Yourself Rich, A Million Bucks by 30 -- among hundreds of other titles at any local bookstore.

My mother had tried numerous 'get rich quick' schemes including pyramid schemes of selling Nu Skin cosmetics, Tupperware and encyclopedias – to our neighbors and friends. Although none of her schemes worked (most often, she lost all of her initial investments), her vision always entailed amassing great wealth in the shortest possible time with the least amount of work.

In the definition of the American Dream by James Truslow Adams in 1931, "life should be better and richer and fuller for everyone, with opportunity for each according to ability or achievement" regardless of social class or circumstances of birth.

Even the Declaration of Independence supported me by saying that "all men are created equal" and that they are "endowed by their Creator with certain inalienable Rights" including "Life, Liberty and the pursuit of Happiness."

So, why wasn't I happy? It was a strange paradox to be an unhappy 'wealthy' American in the happiest country in the world. During my marriage, my husband and I continued to achieve greater material successes – it never seemed like it was enough. – there were always ever-changing fashions, new models of cars, bigger and better luxury properties and unexpected new technological products that were making me dissatisfied and hungering for more.

My Materialistic Stairmaster

Much happiness is overlooked because it doesn't cost anything. - Unknown

I think that my fetish with designer shoes, luxury items and grand displays of wealth such as the Mega mansion had much to do with my idea that these 'things' symbolically would shift me out of my middle class 'unhappy' upbringing and place me into a successful, happy place where my rich, good-looking peers lived.

I think we have all experienced this on some level or another, the longing for a designer dress, expensive artwork or new car. Once we acquire the object of our desires, however, within a few weeks, things go back to normal again. It is like the junky high. And the next time, we will need even more to get the same effect.

My dad is a psychologist so I looked in the Diagnostic and Statistical Manual of Mental Disorders, which categorizes three stages of addiction:

preoccupation/anticipation, binge/intoxication, and withdrawal/negative effect.

These stages are described by constant cravings and preoccupation with obtaining the substance; using more of the substance than necessary to experience the intoxicating effects; and experiencing tolerance, withdrawal symptoms, and decreased motivation for normal life activities.

I must admit that most of my life I have felt these pangs for acquiring possessions and the need for more, especially preoccupation and anticipation of my 'next' purchase. Sometimes these feelings are egged on by the fashion magazines that dictate the 'latest' and greatest must-have trend of the season. But what about the stuff I bought last season? Why don't fashion magazines ever help you wear the clothes you already have in your closet?

Way back in the late 1800s, philosopher Veblen first introduced the notion of "conspicuous consumption" explaining that luxury goods have only one real goal -- to impress other people and create envy. This was most likely describing the behavior of the out-of-control upperclasses of his time that built elaborate monster palaces and gave away diamonds and emeralds as party favors.

Since then, several researchers continue to maintain that luxury goods are incapable of increasing overall happiness. At first, I did not believe that this could be true. Perhaps these researchers have never known the joy of having a **Hermes** Birkin bag.

The problem is that you can really only achieve higher status at the expense of somebody else consuming fewer of those goods, and thus, having a lower status. I guessed this is what was stressing me out in Denmark. Although, I was carrying high status luxury goods like the latest Louis Vuitton duffel bag I rendered little admiration, envy or interest from the Danes.

But it gets worse as people tend to compare their own income and level of luxury goods to the income of relevant others -- which is the well-known "keeping up with the Joneses" idea that I was all too familiar with.

Even if people happen to outperform relative to their friends, the happiness in that 'relative' position is constantly eaten away by income growth. For example, a new s-class Mercedes can only serve as a status symbol for as long as few people can afford it. But with rising income levels, more and more people are able to purchase this luxury vehicle and the Mercedes' luxury goods status is diminished.

That means that you have to work even harder to find an even flashier car that, again, may only keep you in the top dog position for a time. Researchers note that conspicuous consumption is a relentless and dynamic process where constant effort is required to acquire the newest and most desirable things just to preserve one's current status in the future!

This research was hitting home in a big way for me. The idea that I always needed to 'trade up' with my cars and houses was one of the key reasons for my divorce...but how does one change a lifetime of behaviors and patterns and could Danish happiness support this change in me?

I began to see my own patterns. Additional income initially provided me with additional happiness as it enabled me to buy more goods and services. But every time I got more money, I just adapted to the higher income by raising my income aspirations. This is how I was able to spend my entire income on luxury clothes, shoes and bags.

Happiness it seems is much like wearing your favorite perfume. Your olfactory system adapts to the fragrance fairly quickly and you no longer notice the scent anymore. Suddenly you need to use a lot more perfume.

In short, my rising aspirations lowered the happiness I derived from a certain level of income as the joy of additional consumption eventually wore off.

My rising material aspirations eventually lead me to a 'Stairmaster affect', where I constantly adapted my aspiration levels to higher income levels and spending. In the long haul, this caused my happiness to stagnate as confirmed by the aspiration level theory -- happiness is determined by the gap between my aspirations and my actual achievements.

The pursuit of happiness is like a person on a treadmill who has to keep working just to stay in the same place.

When I started researching materialistic tendencies and how they were related to happiness, I found a concept called the 'hedonic treadmill,' a psychological phenomenon that explains why material possessions or reaching major life goals do not make people happier for long periods of time.

When people reach a certain goal or attain a new possession, there is often a burst of happiness. Unfortunately, expectations and material desires often increase with this. After a short period of time, the person returns to the level of happiness he/she was at before the new attainment. So people remain at a relatively stable level of happiness despite changes in fortune or the achievement of major goals. As a person makes more money, expectations and desires rise in tandem, which results in no permanent gain in happiness....

Hmm, this resonated with me and my shopping habits. Why was it that I burned to have the latest, greatest this season IT bag, only to find the bag, stashed away at the back of my closet, six months later?

It seemed as if the intrinsic reward centers in our brains adapt automatically. Regardless of your expectations, if you start drinking $50 bottles of wine instead of $10 bottles, sooner or later the $50 wine will taste like a $15 or even $10 wine.

As a gym-nut, my experience is that this phenomenon is closer to being on a Stairmaster. I was trying to climb a ladder of material success with the idea that this would make me happier.

All of this research I found explained so much to me – about my aspirations, my dreams, values and priorities and how it was all so wrong.

Funnily enough, at the time I was researching all of this, a Hollywood movie was released called "The Joneses." While the U.S. and most of the rest of the world are still in recovery following the financial crisis, it was a good time to release a movie that plays into commercialism, trends, ripple effect and must-haves.

The seemingly perfect Joneses move into the largest McMansion in their American suburb in order to do some 'damage' as the characters played by David Duchovny and Demi Moore characters explain. They are not a real family but actually a carefully crafted marketing/sales unit that creates envy among their neighbors, friends and community. They are not just living the American dream, they are selling it.

Marketing experts have dubbed this kind of viral marketing a meme. A meme is an idea that behaves like a virus. It moves through a population, taking hold in each person it infects. Recent memes could be the must-haves of certain women's fashion movements. My daughter definitely wants a pair of Crocs, strange looking plastic shoes that are available in a wide array of candy colors or Uggs, the uber trendy fur boots.

Admittedly it can sometimes be impossible to not be interested in the newest trend. I even bought a pair of MBT sneakers, supposedly ergonomic shoes that give you a workout while you walk ...

Was I inspired by a shop window, an advertisement, a celebrity endorsement or my trendy neighbor? It's hard to say.

The characters in the film call their approach Lifestyle marketing. People are attracted to other people and their lifestyles – they get 'inspired' and buy the same. Unfortunately, the initial 'high' that you get from your purchase eventually wears off. Then like a diabetic needing the next sugar boost, you search again for the next material item.

In the film, the unsuspecting neighbors get sucked into this vicious cycle egged on by their so-called neighbors. The home of this couple becomes a showroom for all their neighbors who quickly become envious and stressed trying to 'keep up.'

During a business trip to San Diego, I met a medical student who was working as a cab driver to earn extra cash. We were talking about the American dream. The first thing he said to me was the American Dream is about property, specifically owning your own home. I asked him, 'why do you say that?' He replied, "Well it's written in the constitution, life, liberty, property and the pursuit of happiness.."

I laughed out loud. "It's life, liberty and the pursuit of happiness. Property is not in there". I pointed out.

But my med school/cabby friend was not unique. Many Americans, including myself, believe that owning property is the American Dream.

When did the American Dream become synonymous with a center stair colonial? Where did the notion come from and why? And the most important question -- does it lead to happiness?

I have to admit that I spent a great deal of my young adulthood dreaming the American Dream and imagining my life in that storybook dream house. I think American TV had presented that world to me and I desperately clung to it.

A friend of mine and I were discussing our 'stories' and what we dreamed for ourselves. It seemed all of our decisions in life were aimed at this materialistic storybook that we created. Now at age 40, I had to ask, had I achieved it?

I did not. My recent divorce due to my excessive materialism was not part of my storybook and had left a sad imprint on every page. No one adds divorce, joint custody, financial issues to their storybook, it almost seemed unfair. I have a nice home but not the American dream house.

I had not realized my American dream but could it be that I was living the Danish dream? I decided I needed to keep on looking to find the answers and dig into the happiness research.

Why it's So difficult to Change Your Levels of Life Satisfaction

(for better - even if you win the lottery, get a raise or for worse - get into an accident, get paralyzed or lose a limb!)

Life satisfaction or long-term happiness is a complex subject. So, I began my investigation by looking at happiness perspectives and research from economics, psychology, philosophy, and so on to find the answers.

I will start off by tearing down the famous adage— The Secret to a Happy Life is: Be Healthy, Wealthy and Wise. What a crock!

Be Healthy

Every women's magazine has a zillion articles about good body health, different kinds of physical activities and exercise, good nutrition and numerous rest and relaxation techniques.

Again, you would think that being healthy is a major prerequisite to being happy -- every smiling, gorgeous model on the magazine cover looking healthy and fit tells us so. This seems a good time to admit to one of my major issues - I have spent a great deal of my life being stressed about losing weight, taking more spinning classes, kicking my Diet Coke habit, etc.

I always assumed that good health was linked to happiness since one always believed that sick people are miserable and we all do everything possible to keep ourselves far away from the doctor and general hospital. But research shows that people who become disabled have an amazing 30% to 50% recovery in mental well-being and happiness. They have also found young patients who had lost limbs to cancer compared with those who had not experienced similar levels of happiness.

Actually what is linked to unhappiness is our own perceptions of our health. By purely believing that we are healthy (when we are not), we can steer life satisfaction in a positive direction. So no worries, if you are unhealthy but have a great, positive attitude – you can be happy!

Be Wealthy

For much of my life, I have dreamed of being happy by having access to great riches by doing very little: either by somehow finding my 'real' well-to-do parents, marrying an NBA basketball player, inheriting money from a wealthy distant relative or even winning the Danish lottery.

Again researchers have shown me how wrong I have been - that lottery winners, trust fund babies and others who get their money without working for it do not get nearly as much satisfaction from their cash as those of us who earn it the old fashioned way—by working 9 to 5.

Researchers measured brain activity in the striatum, the part of the brain associated with reward processing and pleasure, among two experimental groups: one that had to work to earn money while playing a challenging computer game and another that was rewarded by simply opening sealed envelopes which contained varying amounts of money.

The brains of those who had to work for their money were significantly more stimulated and for a prolonged period of time. The "pleasure factor" registered by those who did not have to work for their money was minimal and short-lived.

What is really scary is that there is so much evidence indicating that people who win the lottery are not happier a year after their success. It's also clear from the body of psychological literature that people obtain a great deal of satisfaction from the work they do.

You often read in the papers that second and third generations who follow successful entrepreneurs and founders of corporations often reveal significant depression, substance abuse and continual marital discord in spite of the great wealth they have inherited.

Some say that it goes back to how the brain is wired. Humans are simply not created to be lottery winners, wealthy slackers or trust fund babies.

Funny enough, some of my most unhappiest friends are people who inherited their wealth. It always seemed like they were struggling with their identities – either trying to hide the wealth they had or proving that they had actually earned it.

Unhealthy versus Wealthy?

I am not really sure why this is but one interesting study that compared happiness levels of people who are NOT healthy (people who have had like serious accidents) and those who ARE wealthy (by like winning the lottery) found NO differences in life satisfaction.

On the day of winning the lottery, happiness for the winners was very high (whew, at least that sounds right) and was significantly lower for the day of the accident for victims. What's interesting is that research showed that once all the 'dust was settled' lottery winners reported the same level of life satisfaction as a group of people who had been injured or paralyzed in an accident.

As it turned out, eventually happiness equalized for both groups.

As for day-to-day joy, the lottery winners found that daily activities like shopping for clothes was less fun than it was for the accident victims.

So an accident victim had more fun shopping for clothes than a state lottery winner! Weird, I often had fantasies of winning big at the LOTTO and having a shopping spree at Neiman Marcus. This apparently would not bring me joy.

I once told my current DH (Danish husband) that if I had ever won the lottery, I would host an Easter Egg Hunt for my girlfriends and inside each beautiful hand-painted egg would be fine jewelry like a diamond tennis bracelet or Tiffany earrings. I know, I know, I have a great imagination and by the way, I have stopped buying lottery tickets.

But what if I earn my wealth, you say, fair and square. That should make me happy, right?

Not really. In the happiness research world, the Easterlin paradox -- also called the 'Frustrated Achievers paradox' is still considered groundbreaking.

It was the first research to show that once your basic needs are met, more money does not increase your life satisfaction. Basically, money can only make a difference in your happiness if you are in a country where you are really struggling – like lacking proper housing, food and access to healthcare.

Easterlin writes that once basic needs are met, the average reported level of happiness does not vary much with national income per person. For example, income per person rose steadily in the United States between 1946 and 1970 but the average person did not get happier.

This is because material aspirations tend to increase proportionately to income over the life cycle and, therefore, measures of happiness decreases with material aspirations. Exactly, as soon as you have more money, you increase expectations.

Wow, so why bother to strive for the next promotion or bonus targets? It occurred to me that this is must be how Danes think and why many of my colleagues never 'aggressively negotiated' for their yearly raise but instead asking for even more holiday (most already had 6 weeks paid holiday).

These studies struck me that most of us were like Weebles when it came to long-term happiness. Weebles were little egg shaped toys that when pulled or pushed, a gravitational force bounced it back to its upright position. Weebles had the 1970's slogan - 'Weebles, wobble but they don't fall down'.

Like the Weebles, long-term happiness had a way of stabilizing itself after a 'wobble' no matter what life circumstance hit it – positive (like winning the lottery) or negative (like getting into an accident).

Be Wise

In a perfect world, college equals success, success equals money and money equals happiness.

Sorry...but there is no data to support this equation. The link between higher education like a college degree and personal greater happiness does not exist. And the same is true for intelligence – being smarter than your neighbor does not make one satisfied with life.

At the micro-level, researchers looked at the results of 23 studies and found no correlation between IQ and happiness. But at the macro-level, they found that an increase in average IQ also meant there was an increase in average happiness in 143 nations.

The famed happiness scientist, Ruut Veenhoven's study concluded that:

Smart people are not happier than their less smart fellow citizens.....

But his study showed that if a country's citizens as a group had better average intelligence than average happiness was also increased for the whole nation. This led me to start thinking about the Danish school system that pays for everyone to get a higher education, not just those who can afford it.

Interesting, delving into the data, told me that I really had been focusing on the wrong stuff. The American dream focused on promises of great happiness by building fortunes via maximizing individual gains. Most of my life, I assumed that great health (with a perfect body), great wealth (with a huge dream mansion and loads of designer shoes) and my college degree (with a high IQ to match) were going to make me happy.

All of these theories support the argument that money does not buy happiness and that the pursuit of money as a way to reach this goal is futile. Good and bad fortunes may temporarily affect how happy a person is, but most people will end up back at their normal level of happiness especially if their peers are able to keep up. How wrong was I.

Part 2 – The Weird but Happy Danes

Hitting a Rut in My Pursuit of Happiness

As with many writers, about one year into this Danish happiness investigation I had somehow gotten off track in my pursuit of Danish happiness and started attracting, sowing and harvesting some totally bad karma, for example: my car got scratched up by some jerk, my newly renovated bathroom became infested with flying ants! (really gross), I had a major fallout with an old friend and am no longer speaking to her...The list goes on and on.

In addition, changes in Danish immigration law had created many unhappy foreigners in Denmark and I have been receiving letters from my Blog readers about this.

Because I wasn't thinking or writing about happiness, I wasn't attracting it either. As I became focused on my daily life, trials and tribulations, I lost focus on what makes me or for that matter Danes happy. Instead, I was focusing on what was not making me happy – what was wrong with everything and everyone, criticizing, analyzing, hyper-analyzing with the idea that it will make it better. It's a slippery slope that is easy to fall into.

This unfortunately is the plague of many expats in Denmark. I can surely empathize with them: It is really difficult to integrate in Denmark, the immigration laws are strict, speaking the language as a foreigner can make you feel like a circus clown, stuff is very expensive (don't get me started on taxes) and the endless days of grey weather can sometimes drive you insane especially after returning from three weeks in sunny Florida.

But I began to realize that negative emotions take up a huge space in our mindsets and positive emotions sometimes take a backseat. For example, we have an incredible vocabulary to describe unhappiness – depression, melancholy, fear, gloom, annoyance, anguish, disturbance, regret, stress, sorrow, sadness, (I've got plenty more).

And it is always easy to find comrades to commiserate in using this immense vocabulary. How many countless conversations do I hear of people complaining about kids, husband, boss, etc.? If you have a problem, it's always easy to find someone, talk and bitch it out. But it's rare that I feel better after the conversation. Instead, many times I feel empty and exhausted.

In addition, some of our heroes in books, film and television are intelligent, negative, mean persons who people 'learn' to like?   Take the popular character *House*, for example, a bitter but ingenious doctor who spits aggressive one-liners at his colleagues and patients. When I was a news journalist, (many years ago), the negative stories were always the most popular and the ones that hit the front page.

And while we all seem to seek happiness, there are so few words to describe the concept and we rarely use them. I can't remember the last time I used the words bliss or joy in everyday conversation.

A worried friend sat me down and made me watch a video based on the book called *The Secret*. While some of the film was a bit corny and focused on materialistic gains, I think the overall message was clear, you attract what you get. Was I attracting problems and negativity? Was I sending an unintelligible message to ants to come and attack my home?

Around that time, I had a funny personal experience with accidently finding Danish style happiness in a Swedish cabin.

The pessimist complains about the rain; the optimist expects it to change; the realist brings

***an umbrella. The Dane loves to get wet,
Sharmi Albrechtsen***

During one fall break after my divorce from the X, my Danish friends arranged a trip to the Swedish woods in Småland and forced me to go. As you know, I had recently been downgraded in my economic circumstances as a single mom and this was also inexpensive way for my buddies to treat me to a much needed weekend away.

If I am being honest, I am more of a city girl than a country girl. I have never been camping and the thought of living in the woods in a rustic cabin does not really appeal to me. I am scared of insects and have phobias about mice. Indeed, I almost burned down a friend's summerhouse by accident one year when I surrounded my bed with mosquito repelling citronelle candles in hopes of not being bitten and one fell over and started a small fire.

So on arriving at the cabin, my fears were realized. It was kind of a dump. Underneath the stove in full view was a mousetrap set and ready to go. Cobwebs with daddy long leg spider families still in them were cottoned up in every corner. The bathroom smelled like poop, even after I cleaned it several times! The bed was stone hard and cramped, the radiator was creaking. Pink fuzzy insulation was peeking out of the cracked walls and ceilings

You can imagine the rest!

I just needed to survive four days I assured myself. I was in survival mode. I ignored all the problems, pretended I did not really hear when someone mentioned that mice had eaten through the living room sofa. Pure and simple, I blocked it out.

The days passed and we were leaving, finally leaving (Thank God). During the last breakfast, everyone at the table was raving about the trip. They simply had the best time ever and weren't the cabin and location fantastic? Ja, ja they all agreed around the table and nodded that the trip was wonderful.

I sat at that breakfast table (fitted with an uncharming brown plastic table cloth) – nearly dumfounded. Come on!!! They can't be serious? Were we on the same holiday? I asked myself incredulously. I barely uttered a word, smiled weakly and said something incomprehensible into my napkin.

I was trying to become a convert to Danish happiness, half glass full etc., etc., but this was too much. When did happiness cross over into delusionalism....I know it seems cruel to say it but if you are so far out from reality then the term delusion – a false belief strongly held in spite of invalidating evidence- sounded like an appropriate description of this crazy talk.

In the car ride home, I asked my friend Mr J about this. Seriously, I said to him how could people think this was a great place?

He looked at me and shook his head, did you really listen to what they said? The Danes around the table were talking about the experiences we had – not focusing on the cabin.

He went on:

Don't you remember we took fantastic walks in the forest and fed the Icelandic horses? One of the days, we woke up to a beautiful snow fall and we created snow men and went sledding. We also had some wonderful meals together, where we baked fresh bread every morning and cooked crispy æbleskivers (Danish donuts) from scratch. What about the great day we had at the Glasriket – we went to the glass museum and then travelled to Kosta Boda where we watched the glassblowers make crystal vases.

Damn it, he was right. Was it possible I actually did have a good time but was determined not to be happy due to preconceived notions and high expectations of only liking 5 star hotels? Unlike delusion, the word pessimism perhaps described my behavior -- a tendency to stress the negative or unfavorable or to take the gloomiest possible view.

It was a funny lesson learned about myself. I might actually like camping. Therefore, I am now open to my next foray into the Swedish forest. What the heck, I may even look into buying a Swedish cabin of my very own. On second thoughts, maybe not. ☺

The cabin incident got me thinking about my attitudes.

After living life in the fast lane, becoming a real life single mom in Denmark was really tough for me because my after tax pay wasn't so high and after paying for my life (rent, food, etc), I had no money to have a 'life'.

I couldn't afford to maintain my expensive habits and although I was beginning to see the light, I needed a bigger push. My former materialistic habits started negatively affecting my image of myself and it made me desire these material possessions even more because they were so out of reach. Yet each time I struggled and bought these 'expensive things' – albeit shoes/handbags/cars – the happiness gained with the item seemed even more short-lived than before and the stress of living beyond my means was unbearable.

I knew my materialistic ways contributed to my second divorce and I figured it was time for a drastic life transformation. But I wasn't really sure how. While the happiness data I had collected was interesting – all it told me was that the stuff I focused on was not making me happy but I still didn't have the answer of what would make me happy.....And the issue about the Danes and their happiness...well, I had not cracked that nut either.

In late 2010, I decided to pull myself together, put together a work plan and start investigating 'real' Danes and the everyday ways that they find gladness and joy.

Oprah's Lifeclass

During that important year, I also reprioritized my values and although I hate to admit it - Oprah's Lifeclass had been a great inspiration. I kept a personal journal and many of the Lifeclass lessons gave me the personal strength to kick my bad habits, change behavior and find happiness for my life in Denmark and contributed to writing this book.

Things I learned in Lifeclass:

·   I realized that I had these 'shadow beliefs' that Tony Robbins talks about. I had made a story that I was doomed to be unhappy in Denmark because I couldn't afford all the material things I was accustomed to. This was holding me back from appreciating what I did have.

·   We were all created to serve some specific function in life and I really did have a purpose – beautifully described by TD Jakes. My purpose was to use my life lessons learned from living an unfulfilling materialistic life and (once I find it) spread the secrets of Danish happiness to others around the world.

Another important lesson for me was when Deepak Chopra talked about living in the present and being happy with the now. This is really one of my daily mantras- I used to always obsess about the next 'purchase' ....and now I spend more time in the present.

In Denmark we have something called Hygge in Danish – which is finding simple and cozy moments EVERY day. Enjoying fresh flowers, sunshine or lighting candles...making sure I always have a sit down family dinner at the table (even its just takeout sushi) .

Flush out my Ego. Ego is any identification with things, such as your possessions or social status and "Understanding the ego is having the awareness of your true self and your ego self." Being aware of my ego and the fact that SHE creeps up on me, especially when I start to identify myself with stuff – my Gucci bag does not love me back!

Another one of my favorites is the lesson: ' You become what you believe', I really loved Jim Carey's story and the importance of having vision, imagination and belief in yourself. I used those techniques and they seemed to work.

The question: 'Was I telling myself a story that I would be unhappy (in Denmark)?' Much of my life class exercises helped me to see my story, the stories of the

Danes around me and how our lives and experiences were very different. I must admit it was difficult to find the real truths under all of the cultural contexts, different points of view and values.

Oh, Happy Danes

Are the Danes really the happiest people in the world? I am asked time and time again. And I must admit, ergghh, ahh, well the thing is, it really depends on what your definition of the word happiness is. The literal Danish translation of the word used in the happiness surveys is 'tilfreds' which is loosely translated as content.

Some of you will say, ah ha! I knew they weren't really happy, just content.

But you see I must argue that in many ways, contentment, which can be defined as the state of being satisfied, is closely associated with the concept of happiness. In Positive Psychology social scientists study what contributes to living 'the good life', or what people need to do in order to have increased positive moods, pleasures, optimistic attitudes and outlook and overall satisfaction with their life.

So does overall satisfaction with your life mean that you are happy? I believe so and I think most of you would agree with me.

In the spirit of applied mathematics, let's start with the lifetime happiness equation, created by noted psychologist and founder of Positive Psychology Martin Seligman:

H is your overall level of happiness, S is your biological set range (the happiness level you are genetically born with), C is the influence of current life events, and V represents those factors under your voluntary control. $H=S+C+V$

Inspired by his work but crap at math, I will try to explain it in my own terminology. Since baked goods play such an important role in Denmark, I shall refer to it as the Happiness Recipe instead.

Sharmi's Danish Happiness Recipe

Happiness = Self+Life+Choices

The idea is that while you can't really change your happiness genes, but you can do things to maximize your overall position, ie. increase your happiness by playing around with the other factors.

Self - This may be a harsh reality for some of you to accept, but just as a 'diabetes' can be inherited, you also inherit a level of happiness that you will always bounce back to. All people, including Danes, have this biological set point.

With regards to the rest of the recipe, it is easy to see why the Danes are tipping the happiness scales and are indeed content with their lives. The Life ingredient – life conditions in Denmark, ie. the welfare state make it very palatable to be here.

The Danish welfare state has a high rate of economic growth and a high standard of living to match. In Denmark, citizens are financially insured, e.g. in case of illness and old age, so this relieves many of the stresses and strains felt in other countries.

In my opinion, another aspect of Life could be weather, sunshine or even taxes.

I spent nearly one year studying Danish habits with regards to Self, Life as well as Choices – that is 'chosen' activities.

These activities are within your control and increasing the number and intensity of activities will tip your happiness scales and have little to do with money – making it or spending it.

Danes prioritize these activities and work-life balance is a way of life there.

Self is the happiness level you are genetically born with

Contemporary understanding of happiness is that a material portion of your outlook is largely set (this is called the happiness "set point" theory and you can blame genetics for that) and surprisingly life circumstances generally play a smallish role.

Experts say that from an evolutionary point of view we should expect our biological happiness state to bounce back to normal levels each time something positive or negative affects us. So the question naturally arises, are the Danes born with a happiness gene?

Visitors always ask about the paradox of unfriendly, icy Danes who claim to be extremely happy. I hosted some friends from the UK a while back. While we were lunching at the MASH (Modern American Steak House) in Charlottenlund, they couldn't help but notice that our waiters were aloof and a bit stony-faced as we tried to charm them with our wit and cheery smiles.

My foreign friend flippantly commented, 'Hmm, these Danes don't seem very happy,' and of course that was my cue to try to explain this strange paradox. When one visits the country of the happiest people of the world, one cannot assume that happiness is interconnected with friendliness.

Danes have more subdued and more consistent, levels of positive affect as compared to Americans[iii]. Although there are little or no differences cross-culturally on intrinsic personality types such as introverts or extroverts, personality traits such as optimism and self-esteem are usually a product of one's environment, upbringing, social groups as well as genetics.

There is little data on the personality types of Danes; however, there exists data that suggests that Danes report more moderate changes in mood than Americans.[iv]

This could suggest a different, less emotional personality type for Danish people compared to Americans. While there is a large amount of data in the U.S. on self-esteem and different genders and ages, there is little data from Denmark to compare.

In the U.S., people feel stronger feelings of positive emotions and have higher positive and negative affect and spikes in happiness. People from the U.S. are much more prone to having more peak experiences—more intense feelings of joy and excitement.

Danes show disdain when watching American game shows such, "Extreme Makeover," when the new American homeowners scream and cry with delight when shown their new bathrooms and kitchens.

"I don't understand why they have to freak out so much, it's so embarrassing," said a Danish friend Miss G. "It's just a kitchen, for God's sake."

Recently there was a popular game show that brought Americans over to Denmark who were seeking knowledge about their Danish heritage. It was called Alt for Denmark and featured Americans doing crazy activities like walking on tightropes across Nyhavn harbor area to gain points and more information about their distant relatives. Danes enjoyed watching Americans get all gooey-eyed about their Danish ancesters, laughing at their emotional outbursts.

Another American friend who had recently lost her mother, went to play golf with some Danish friends and mentioned that she might not play so well because of her sorrow and grief.
Her comment was met with unsympathetic and pitiless replies like, 'C'mon, grow up and get over it. Everyone has to die.'

On the one side, this kind of attitude may seem harsh: it may be brought on by the long, tough winters and the Viking heritage. Whatever the cause though, by having a more moderate and consistent mood, Danes are able to keep content and satisfied for longer periods of time.

I have worked on this mood regulation for about 2 years to see if I could alter biology and I must say 'letting things go' has given me great rewards including better sleep, happier relations with my family and friends and fewer days with tears and *Ben and Jerry* ice cream.

Beautiful Homogenous People

Another biological advantage Danes could have is that most are considered very attractive.

Shiny Happy People (Holding Hands….). R.E.M must have been to Denmark when they were inspired to write those lyrics. I think that one key reason that could lead to Denmark's high happiness ratings is its extremely homogenous population. Danes are exceptionally the 'same' on almost all levels— racially, culturally, and socioeconomically.

It's hard to say whether this leads to happiness. There is conflicting data whether homogeneity of race and culture leads to happiness and some of this data is skewed because of high race/culture inequality in developing countries where there is also social unrest.

However, Denmark has a unique cultural identity where equality and homogeneity are an integral aspect. Denmark's population consists of 90.1% Danish people. One possibility is that it binds the country in a common cultural and ideological state, creating a stronger sense of cultural identity. Another consideration is that it could lead to less conflict.

As an Asian-American, I must admit it has been somewhat difficult to just 'blend' in.

Being a dark, long-haired, short and curvy body type is damned difficult in a country filled with long, lean legged natural blondes.

My early days of shopping here, led to despair as I could never find jeans that were not too long, jackets that didn't have arms made for monkeys and a mini-skirt that actually sat correctly – above my knee.

Shopping for make-up was always a torture, since the only tan/bronze colored foundation they would have in stock was Dark Espresso. I never understood the retail shop buyer who I guess had to carry a range of makeup shades, decided that there was no color between Porcelain Alabaster and Dark Espresso.

Does beauty lead to happiness? And could that be a reason that Danes are happier? Walking down the streets of Copenhagen, it is hard not to notice that people are objectively better looking (tall, athletic/slim with good features and blonde hair) compared to other countries.

Visitors to Denmark almost always remark about the 'good looks' of the Danes both men and women. Our recently elected prime minister, Helle Thorning-Schmidt is petite, blonde and very stylish and there have been suggestions that she received considerably more media coverage than her adversaries because of her 'photogenetics'.

My suspicions that Danes are top of the beauty food chain are now also supported by recent evidence from the BeautifulPeople.com website. The site which started in Denmark 2002, last month launched globally to provide good looking people worldwide a dating site just for them. Apparently, the site rejected nearly 1.8 million unattractive people from 190 countries in its first two weeks of launch.

From the total number of hopefuls, only 360,000 new members have been admitted. Interestingly, the Scandinavians monopolized the top spots with the most successful applicants from Sweden, Denmark, Norway and applicants from Germany and the UK among the least successful.

Indeed the highest 'hit' rates came from Norwegian women (76 percent approval ratings), Swedish men (65 percent) and Danish men (40 percent) who were easily accepted in. For some reason, the ratings for Danish women were not available...strange! Since I am confident they would fare well.

To become a member of the dating site, applicants are required to be voted in by existing members of the opposite sex. According to the creators of the website, 'the vote is fair and democratic'. In addition, the website says they (BeautifulPeople) do not define beauty, it simply gives an accurate representation of what society's ideal of beauty is as decided by the members.

What is interesting is not that beautiful Danes only want to date each other but that numerous studies support that the best relationships are made from people who are alike, come from similar backgrounds and educations and even hair color.

This is a trait that I noticed a lot in Denmark – opposites rarely attracted. Indeed most people appeared to be the happiest with other Danes from their neighborhood, school or even sports club.

One Danish friend Ms G summed it up by saying, 'A husband should be like your best playmate from school, or brother. He should live down the street and be able to bike you to the library.

Life is the influence of current life events

Many Danes claim that Denmark is a classless society which makes conditions for everyone here great. It is kind of true, there aren't severe class distinctions. The poor get helped, the rich and upwardly mobile get taxed heavily and everyone gets squashed into a big, fat middle class. This ranks Denmark as having the world's highest level of income equality and has one of the world's highest per capita income countries in the world.

Denmark follows the Nordic model of a mixed economy, which has a large welfare state, a gigantic public expenditure and a universal social system (including free university/higher education and health care for all), financed by taxes and not by social contributions.

Denmark has an interesting kind of hybrid economy. Although Denmark has a huge welfare state, it also fiercely embraces many free market ideas. The unemployment benefits are generous, but it's also very easy to fire people. That keeps the economy nimble. Employers can get rid of workers when they don't need them and hire them back quickly when they do.

To pay for this large welfare state, the Danish tax burden is heavy and sometimes crippling to the working stiff. With income tax averaging from 50 to 68 percent, car taxes of more than 180 percent and a stiff 25 VAT (value added tax) added to all purchases – it can be sometimes difficult to bring home any bacon.

The Weather Mystery: Cold weather, wind, darkness. Bloody hell, how can one be happy?

Another interesting life condition is the weather here in Denmark. I admit I had taken the sun for granted for most of my life. When you live in Washington DC the summer heat swelters down on you with a combination of sticky, gooey humidity – that makes you feel like a donut that's been steamed and then dipped into a sugar glaze. Most summers left me running with my frizzy hair for my air conditioned apartment, car and even God forbid workplace- anywhere to get respite from the heat.

So at first, I welcomed the cool, brisk weather and the weak sunlight in Denmark. That is until my first winter....

My first winter in Denmark is frozen stiff in my brain because after a few weeks in January, I felt a sick depression and started to weep uncontrollably for no particular reason. Then, I realized I hadn't seen or felt the sun for five days straight.

In 2010, Copenhagen had 1,539 sunshine hours, this compared to U.S.'s sunniest city, Phoenix with 3,752 hours and the least sunniest, Seattle with 2,049 hours. Denmark also has long, dark winters. On the shortest days in Denmark, the sun rises at 9:30 a.m. and will set at 3:30 p.m. By contrast, the summer in Denmark is super long with the sun rising at 3:30 a.m. and the sun setting at 10 p.m.

Once I actually missed the night totally. I walked into a disco around 9.30 pm and it was still light and when we were finished partying Danish style with a midnight snack served at 2 a.m.- it was still sunny outside.

The weather here can get you down. Because of the long winter seasons in Denmark there are many cases of seasonal affect disorder (SAD). This is where a person's mood is greatly decreased to the point of depression when the seasons change, especially to a dark winter. One study showed that the rate of seasonal affect disorder was over 12 percent in Denmark.[v]

The Danes have the weirdest invention known to man, called a Light therapy box, which basically looks like a 'glow in the dark' toaster. Many Danes suffering from

SAD sit in front of these lightboxes for at least an hour a day. Apparently it mimics the sun and affects brain chemicals linked to mood.

Denmark, Finland and some U.S. states with higher happiness levels also tend to have higher suicide rates. For example, Utah is ranked number 1 in life satisfaction but has the ninth-highest suicide rate, whereas New York, ranked 45th in satisfaction, has the lowest suicide rate in the U.S.

Is it the long, dark winters that cause the problem?

It seems misery loves company and researchers believe that depressed people may become distressed by seeing other people content and happy. Sadly, this may mean that increasing happiness by reducing economic inequality could paradoxically produce more suicides as a "side effect."

In the book, the "Geography of Bliss," author Erik Weiner travels the world to find the most happy and unhappy countries (for some reason, he skipped Denmark ☺). On his website, he asks readers to name their paradise or 'happy places' but many of these places were warm, tropical vacation spots.

If Americans travelled to the 'real' happy countries: Denmark, Iceland, Quatar and Switzerland, would they consider themselves to be in paradise?

From a sociological perspective the term paradise, is "often used to reference a society (whether it be hypothetical or otherwise) whose organizational features serve to create a harmonious, luxurious development of the psychological, physiological and creative natures of mankind.

As such, a society, continent or planet so constructed, naturally provides a suitably nourishing and convivial social and educational formula that would nourish and grow unconditional joy and happiness within that populace

The word paradise entered European languages from the Persian root word "Pardis" which was the name of a beautiful garden enclosed between walls. In this sense, paradise existed on earth and was a place that uplifted the human spirit and seemed attainable (sounds like my backyard actually).

This is where Hollywood and fiction writers stepped in with their version of paradise: Caribbean style island with abundant gorgeous white sandy beaches, spectacular and colorful sunrises, crystal clear water, sunny weather always, fresh fruit trees and palm trees on every corner. When you 'google' *paradise* every photo showing paradise shows images that emphasize this.

Surprisingly, weather and environment are not factors in a person's happiness. Research supports that people have the same levels of happiness when the sun is shining and when it's fairly warm to those suffering through a dark, dreary winter.

Apparently we adapt to good weather fairly quickly so, much like my Gucci bag, a series of sunny days have less happiness value and therefore less appeal.

It seems to me that paradise on earth as we know it does not exist, at least it seems quite conflicted. And moving to a tropical location would certainly not lead to long-term happiness.

Some of the most beautiful and paradise-like locations seem to be the most unhappiest with high rates of poverty, social inequity and crime and the countries that have long dark winters with no sun, no palm trees and very few or no white sandy beaches are rated the happiest.

Religion in Denmark

While the research with regards to religion and happiness is a mixed bag, I think it is fair to quote Dr. Seligman who says that religion has a moderate effect towards affecting happiness mainly because the relation of hope for the future and religious faith fights despair.

Danes have an interesting relationship with religion as I see it, as it is mostly an excuse to *partaay*. While nearly 83% of Danes are affiliated with the Evangelical Lutheran Church of Denmark, less than 10% of this group regularly attends church services and unless you have booked an 'event' – baptism, wedding, confirmation- - most Danes only go to church at Christmas and maybe Easter.

Most consider themselves not to be religious but I have to counter that maybe they don't go to church but it does not stop them from celebrating the religious holidays.

When my daughter was baptized at a local church outside of Copenhagen, the pastor asked me if I had been baptized. When I said I had been confirmed at age 13, he said it did not 'count' and I should consider being baptized at age 32 so that my soul would not end in 'limbo' when I died.

Okay, I just wanted to talk about whether he was going to have chicken or beef at the reception...was not prepared for the 'lost soul discussion' or an adult baptism. Lutheranism is based on the principle of faith as a means of Salvation, and most Danes admit that they were only baptized as a "precautionary measure."

And here comes the taxes again... under the nation's Constitutional monarchy, there is no separation of Church and State. Although there is freedom of religion, the sitting monarch must be a member of the state church. The church also receives subsidies from the Government—members of the church must pay 1% of their income in taxes, regardless of whether or not they are active. A whopping 90 percent of Danes pay this tax.

Outsiders find it extraordinarily strange that a nation whose residents pay religious taxes have so little interest in religious practice.

There is clear evidence that shows people who are religious have a deeper sense of happiness and despite the lack of religious fervor in Denmark, Danes are well known for their celebration of religious holidays, especially all of the Easter holidays and Christmas; here comes the 'party' element.

It is so integrated that they even have 'religious' beers – both for Easter and Christmas the Carlsberg Brewery produces spicy beers that contain slightly more alcohol than the regular recipe. The Danish bakeries also play a role by making sure that most religious holidays have a corresponding baked goodie to match.

One of my favorites is the Fastelavn bøller or in English a shrovetide bun, which is a round sweet flaky roll usually covered with chocolate icing and filled with whipped cream.

Fastelavn which is the name for Carnival in Denmark is either the Sunday or Monday before Ash Wednesday. Fastelavn evolved from the Roman Catholic tradition of celebrating in the days before Lent, but after Denmark became a Protestant nation, the holiday became less specifically religious and more based on enjoyment and fun. Again, I never really understood Fastelavn and when I asked around most Danes had not a clue either.

One year, my daughter demanded that I buy her a Fastelavns ris (a bunch of twigs with candy bunches tied to it) – 'because all the other kids were getting one' but when I asked her what religious or even historical significance it had – she, nor any other Dane that I asked. could answer.

That evening I made a deal with her – do some research, make a powerpoint presentation explaining the holiday and the Fastelavns ris significance and I would indeed buy her one.

So here is her summary:

Fastelavn is similar to Halloween in that children dress up in costume in order to ward off evil spirits. They also play a game called 'hit the cat out of the barrel', which is somewhat similar to hitting a piñata. The Danes use a wooden barrel, which is full of candy and sometimes oranges and has the image of a cat on it. Historically there was a real black cat in the barrel (how sad!), and beating the barrel was superstitiously considered a safeguard against evil.

Another popular Danish custom (especially among the children) is the "fastelavnsris", with which children ritually flog their parents to wake them up on the morning of Fastelavns Sunday.

Flogging your parents? What in the world?!

Again, here is another Danish holiday ritual with its knickers in a twist. No one is really sure where this custom really originated from – the more serious one is that after the reformation, unusually pious people would flog their children on Good Friday as a symbol of the sufferings of Christ or the fertility ritual where Danish bachelors and virgins "bid each other goodmorning" by playfully flogging each other. How nice.

Regardless, the modern day Danish family decorates these 'flogging' instruments with feathers, ribbons, egg-shells, storks, little figures of babies and candy.

And this is the case for many Danish religious holidays and their corresponding rituals – the Danes are casual about the actual religious sentiment but focus on the social and community element.

One so-called religious holiday that specifically makes me chuckle – is Store Bededag, translated literally as Big Prayer Day which is a Danish holiday celebrated on the 4th Friday after Easter. It is actually a collection of Christian holy days consolidated into one day, so it really has no specific religious significance and there are very few traditions associated with it and certainly little praying. Of course, it does involve 'eating' specifically – varme hveder buns are special cardamom scented rolls that are baked and consumed on this day. They might as well call this day the Big Bun Day since more baking and eating is done than praying.

Christmas in Denmark, Nearly a Cult-like Fervor

The biggest religious festival in Denmark, hands down, is Christmas. It lasts the entire month of December and it is really a time to see Danish happiness in true ACTION. Kids here watch at least two Christmas TV shows a day, all children expect the traditional Danish calendar gift wall, which normally requires me to find 24 very small, creative, high quality, individually wrapped (but still inexpensive) gifts, in addition to advent gifts that are given each Sunday in December and finally the gifts on Christmas Eve.

This is one of happiest months of the year in Denmark and even strangers will smile at you – 'at the Christmas market in Tivoli'.

Hygge and Christmas are also closely related in Denmark. The Danish word for "Christmas" is Jul, from the Old Norse Jól akin to the English Yule.

As such the word does not refer to the birth of Christ, but instead to an ancient pagan winter feast. Which also means – Christmas is for everybody!

Its customs have, of course, changed over the years, but it has always been part of Scandinavian culture. It meant so much to the Scandinavians that in order to convert them, the church had to adopt their holiday into Christianity, which is the actual origin of Christmas.

In many countries Christmas is celebrated on the 25th of December, but in Denmark, and in the other Scandinavian countries, it is held on the 24th.

On December the 24th, the family gathers. The morning can be spent in various ways but most often it is the time when preparations are made for the evening and pretty much all Danish families eat the EXACT same meal.

Juleaften (Danish for Christmas Eve) or Yule Eve starts around 6 p.m. when a traditional dinner is served. The menu is:

• White (boiled) and sugar-browned potatoes, red cabbage and brown sauce (gravy) accompanying either roast duck or goose depending on the size of the family. Some families enjoy a special Danish version of roast pork, called flæskesteg complete with crackling.

• For dessert, ris á l'amande is served, a name that suggests a French origin - but it is Danish. Sometimes it is confused with rice pudding, since they share the main ingredient (rice). Ris á l'amande needs to be prepared a day in advance, and then on serving, chopped almond and vanilla can be added, among other things. It is served cold, with hot cherry sauce. An unchopped almond is also added and hidden in the rice. The person who finds it in his portion receives a marzipan pig.

Afterwards, the candles on the Christmas tree are lit and the family dance around it singing Christmas songs and carols and subsequently exchange presents. My X husband jokingly said this was the 'pagan ritual of the evening,' since neither the tree nor the dancing have religious significance.

I love Danish Christmas, it literally takes up the whole month with activities, baking, decorating, parties, socializing and of course, HYGGE.

This is important because in December it gets dark here around 4pm and if you weren't busy with Christmas 'whohas' then you would probably go straight to bed.

The problem is I am normally coerced into a Danish 'cabin' with all the Danish relatives. Even though my parents are Hindu, I was Christian and went to midnight mass. I grew up with my own special Christmas traditions. We celebrated Christmas with a formal dinner - dressed up in fine clothes and had a nice meal with Royal Albert porcelain, crystal candelabras, fresh roses on the table, etc.

My happy Danish family-in-laws, well, they are definitely more casual. As my work colleague put it,

Danes are perpetually relaxed....so it's jeans, long sleeve t-shirts and a duck on the bar-b for me every year. While the great barbeque on the 24th will get me through the evening (trying to forget the need for linen napkins), I guess my worst torture will be the Danish Christmas lunch (Julefrokost) afterwards.

My yearly run through the Danish culinary gauntlet is when strange food concoctions are forced on me for hours and where it becomes apparently obvious that I am not a happy Dane. I guess I provide an annual giggle to my Danish in-laws as they pass me dishes that I cannot pronounce, would never be able to cook, nor can force myself eat.

Seriously? Smoked eel, five different kinds of herring, piping hot liverwurst pâté, pickled pigs head (and feet), a pot of freshly made lard...plus a nasty and stinky cheese that is nicknamed 'grandpa Ole.' -- I guess because it smelled like him? Luckily, Danish kids are not daring when it comes to julefrokost, so we share a plate of Danish meatballs and call it a day. I normally wash it down with a glass of shnapps which has a similar taste to (what I think) gasoline would taste like...

If I put aside all my jokes and petty comments, I must admit that generally Christmas in Denmark is pretty amazing and special. I have slowly been warming up to traditional Danish Christmas recipes. I have already created a new family favorite warm æbelskiver (Danish donuts) stuffed with ice cream and served with raspberry coulis- I call it æbelscoop.. Normally these pancake balls are served fresh from the oven with a dusting of powdered sugar and some jam, but my new creation allows me to serve them as a dessert rather than an afternoon snack. Haha!

I have also started making and preserving handmade Danish paper Christmas ornaments. These 'decorations' were always a mystery to me – a paper ornament (!?) To me an ornament is glass or wooden so that it survives storage, year after year. In the past my Danish paper ornaments even after my best effort always look a bit smashed, dirty and faded and even torn. How did the Danes do it? Individual boxes for each ornament, they say. It actually works.

I must admit that the Danish attitude towards religious holidays and tradition is refreshing where the focus is on community, kinship and brotherly love (which is done through dancing, beer drinking and baking breads) instead of all the hell, purgatory and confessions of sin that comes with other religious activities. It certainly adds to the happiness equation in an important way.

Marriage and Relationships in Denmark

Marriage/relationship is one of the strongest indicators of happiness according to decade's worth of research.

Around Valentine's Day 2013, I was sad to see another one of my dear American friends nursing a broken heart after a tough break up with a Danish man. I have to sympathize with her plight – as I know it can be rough.

Especially because Danes are notorious for being pretty cold hearted and moving on (really quickly!) when the love is gone....But what makes these Nordic people so tough when it comes to the affairs of the heart? Why do they choose flight instead of fight? And does it contribute to happiness?

The divorce rate in Denmark has always been a high but steady 40 percent but now it seems less couples are getting married as well. Experts suggest that a combination of factors have led the figure to decline since 2008, including the financial crisis, a parting from tradition, seeing friends with bad divorces and growing up with parents that have divorced.

A special feature of the Danish welfare model is also that the welfare system is not linked to the family. Rather, it tends to be based on a person's need and his or her role in the job market.

So the old fashioned breadwinner is now replaced by households with two incomes. This has contributed to a 'democratization' of access to divorce (nearly everyone can afford to be single again), particularly for women and people with low income.

When Oprah was visiting Denmark in 2009, she had a funny discussion with a Danish woman about divorce rates and why they were so high...

Oprah: You don't need a man to take care of you.
Danish woman: No.
Oprah: And when you don't need a man to take care of you...
Danish woman: Exactly.
Oprah: ...you are with a man just because you...
Danish woman: Exactly.
WINFREY: ...you want to be.

And there it is in a perfect, tiny nutshell. One of the things that leads to a happy Danish life is a good marriage/relationship and you may have to pass through a few partners before you find Mr or Mrs Right. And people here are not willing to settle.

While this topic deserves its own book (no worries, I am working on it!). I have observed that this may be due to a non-existent dating culture in Denmark. People here hook up really fast, take the plunge and then find out months/years later after having moved in together that 'hey, he wasn't the right guy'. I have a divorced Danish friend in her 40s who has moved 5 times (with a different guy) in the last 2 years...

She is not an exception. Actually if I had to characterize them, I would have to label Danes as serial monogamists. They have many sexual partners in their lifetime, but only one at a time. He or she will seemingly form what looks like a lasting commitment to one person, but the commitment is usually pretty short-lived and only lasts if it is still enjoyable and convenient.

I sometimes think that Danish media culture supports serial monogamy as single people are often portrayed as 'freaks'. Watch the Danish program 'Singelliv' – the Single Life in English and it is a pretty scary reality show about insane, tattooed, partygoers who swing from partner to partner in a drunken, tacky stupor.

Unlike the American Sex and the City that explored and promoted singles dating, friendships and relationships in a sexy and sophisticated fashion – Singelliv scares people into monogamy....Get into a relationship, quick! The trailer might as well scream....or you will end up like these weirdos.

Many Danes that I have spoken to take a pragmatic approach to relationships, marriage and the children that they share. Some go on holidays with their ex-husbands/wives and even hold Christmas, birthdays together. That way the children keep a sense of family although the parents are no longer together.

Danish philosopher, Søren Kierkegaard summed it up – 'better well-hung (to death) than ill wed'

That said, often, a person leaves their partner or husband or wife and soon after (like days) is presenting the new partner to friends and family. They say the best way to *get over someone*, is to *get under someone else.*

Two weeks after my separation (months before the divorce was final), Mr.X was sporting his new long legged blonde Danish girlfriend to our friends, family and even introducing *her* to our daughter.

While, I must admit, it was painful to watch causing me many tears and seeking refuge with my favorite boys - Ben and Jerry.- to ease my pain and prevent me from gaining 10 pounds, I also jumped into a new relationship fairly quickly. I think part of my reasoning was that I didn't want to look like a 'loser'. If he could find my replacement so quick, so could I, I told myself.

But was it too quick? Did we throw in the towel too soon.

Perhaps, studies show that 2nd (67 percent) and 3rd marriages (73 percent) fail as well. But I guess it was fun while it lasted.

In some ways, love and marriage in Denmark have become a revolving door – and even the lawmakers are supporting the trend by looking at ways to make divorce even easier.

I have always been fascinated with the freedom that Danes have in their love relationships and marriages. Their prioritization of individual choice is what makes their culture very unique but also successful in finding love and happiness in their lives.

It is a breath of fresh air compared to the constraints of the old 'ball and chain' – I am used to from the USA, where the norms of marriage and divorce are often times set in stone and often feel they are from the stone ages as well.

Danish author and sexologist Sara Skaarup has written the book "Kærlighedskontrakten" or the Love Contract in which she outlines 'The Dynamic relationship' – a NEW style of open marriage that allows for other sexual partners but requires full transparency, rules of engagement and even 'veto' powers for both husband and wife.

I had a chance to speak with her and she was happy to share her experiences with my readers.

She says today most people know of only 2 options – Open Marriage, which are typically conceived to have no limits, no safety or security and the Traditional Monogamy which often is practiced is binding, inflexible and does not necessarily promote personal growth.

But now there is the Dynamic Relationship a new Danish hybrid model to marriage. This type of marriage has 'free passes and extramarital perks' as long as both parties agree to certain terms and conditions. Sometimes the relationship is closed, sometimes its open regarding of what suits the couple at the time. It is a modern way of looking at marriage and family — it is growing in popularity in Denmark .... and I must admit it is pretty intriguing!

Sara Skaarup story begins with a personal marital crisis. Sara Skaarup remembers the evening when she and her husband were sitting in their living room and staring at each other with hurt and jealosy. As the conversation unfolded, it appeared that both of them had flirted, kissed and fondled other people during their 10-year marriage but kept it a secret.

The painful confessions that night would prove to be a defining moment for the couple's future life. Many couples would consider divorce or marriage counseling but she did not feel that those were the answer they needed.

Sara Skaarup grew up in Jutland, Denmark in what she describes as a safe nuclear family. She has been married for more than 10 years and has two young children.

"My husband is the man of my life and he understands my potential to grow. We have a great confidence and honesty, and he has witnessed much of my adult life,' she said.

But I wanted to design my life, I wanted to have the ability to have intimate relationships with more people, she says. And most importantly, keep my marriage.

She created the concept Love Contract as a way for couples to have the best of both worlds – by removing some of the guilt and shame associated with affairs and yet keeping the marriage and family together in a sustainable way.

She says that agreement is the most important part of the contract. The model works well when both parties agree that 'yes' they still consider each other primary lovers – or 'no' that they are not lovers but still have an important relationship with each other.

Sara Skaarup warns that the Love Contract is not a medicine or elixir for all problematic marriages and that it is 'not as easy as it sounds'.

'You have to learn to be happy that your husband will change, grow and even flourish under the influence of another woman,' she says.

On the other hand, you too will grow. Other people we are attracted to, have something we can learn from, and through the relationship with them can we can learn about ourselves.

'It has made me wiser about myself, and it's a relief not to experience the artificial divide between being fully present as a woman in a relationship and possess an erotic energy,' she says.

Although the couple through time has allowed each other to be with others, intimacy remains a key word in their relationship. Intimacy for them that they are honest and do what they say, and they emphasize the value of being in solidarity and stand by each other.

"I'm not trying to overthrow marriage and I don't think that this works for everyone "she says. 'But I hope all couples at least have the conversation about it.'

Her family's home is what she describes as a sacred zone. Here they live a very traditional family life, where time is dedicated to the two children and the desire to give them a stable and healthy childhood.

The children do not experience that suddenly there is a strange man or woman in the bedroom nor do they hear their parents talk about other partners.

Will she encourage her children to follow her Love Contract?

"No, my children have to find their own way of living. But I will surely advise them to go for living their love life according to their open heart and standard rather then just following norms – what form it then takes in less important, she says.

However in the name of love, one of the great strides that Denmark has also made is legalizing same sex marriages and allowing gays to adopt children. So hopefully these couples can turn the tide and maybe put the love, commitment and longevity back in marriage.

Danes spend a great deal of time focusing on their children. But research has shown that children themselves, sorry to say (and as cute as they are), do not equate to daily happiness. Indeed, they increase stress; families with children experience a higher stress level than those who do not.

In Denmark, you can take your child everywhere with you and it is encouraged. Even the finest restaurants have highchairs, nappy changing facilities and will gladly make a kid's meal.

However, on a long term contentment level, children and family are important. I also believe that children provide an important mechanism on Danish society for friendships, networking and other types of community activities.

Therefore, family life is an essential part of living in Denmark. Most relationships and networks are centered around the family here. Sending your child to a boarding school is unheard of and would have to be explained in-depth -- how could any parent do such a thing!

Access to Good Food and Eat to Live

While there are many wonderful and great things about the Danes, their culture and country – one of the worse conditions of living in Denmark is a lack of easy access to well-priced produce, agriculture and food stuffs.

Honestly, with the heavy rains and snow and short summer season, most fruits and vegetables are imported from far away Spain. Most of the time, these unripe veggies go from unripe to rotten within a few days on the kitchen counter. As for locally produced vegetables – we have cabbage, potatoes and well, more cabbage.

The low number of Danish restaurants located around the world probably makes that point quite clear. Traditional Danish food is about heavy meats or fried fish with brown sauce and boiled potatoes or open faced sandwiches.

Even in Denmark itself, the traditional Danish fare is hard to come by and these days a host of chefs have blended the traditional heavy recipes into lighter and fresher fusion fare, but this is mostly to inspire the home chef.

But you know that Denmark is full of paradoxes.... the most recent being that *Restaurant* Magazine named the best restaurant in the world -- NOMA which is located in Copenhagen. The name is a concatenation of the two Nordic words "no' from Nordisk" (Nordic) and "ma' from the word mad" (food), and the restaurant is known for its reinvention and interpretation of the Nordic Cuisine.

I have been there and the food is, well, really creative. For example, they serve live shrimp and forest ants, and I heard that the chefs use the Norwegian army's survival guide for finding edible roots, fungus, moss, bark, leaves and insects from the Danish forests to integrate in their recipes.

But saying that the New Nordic cuisine created at Noma and the host of daughter restaurants birthed by the Danish equivalent to Jamie Oliver, Claus Meyer, is **Danish food** is just wrong. As my husband says, 'it is food made from things you foraged in Denmark' but that do not make it Danish food.'

At my daughter's international school day, children are asked to bring a typical dish from their heritage. Since half the school is Danish, the organizers ended up with thousands of frikadelle (fried Danish meatballs). Where was the New Nordic cuisine on that day? Here's one thing I am sure of, there was nothing on the buffet table that came from the Noma cookbook.

Another issue that makes wonderful eating difficult in Denmark is the tax system. A good friend brings home suitcases full of Danish bacon from her trips to

England. This was no ordinary bacon but back bacon prepared from Danish boneless pork loin.

She brings it back because for some reason it was cheaper to buy Danish bacon in the UK than it was in Denmark. In addition, it seemed the good quality Danish bacon and ribs are all being exported to countries abroad. Those of us who have lived anywhere outside of Scandinavia or Japan know that Denmark is probably one of the most expensive places in the world to live. All food starts with a 25 percent VAT charge and recently the government imposed a larger tax burden on sodas that makes buying beer cheaper than buying a Coke. I always have to cringe a little when I see that butter imported all the way from New Zealand is half the price of Danish Lurpack butter.

To speak about Danish food culture here is a difficult thing. Danes actually believe they eat better than they actually do (Check the AOK: in Copenhagen alone there are more than 1,000 kebab shops, hotdog stands and pizza joints compared to 100 Danish restaurants)

I'm not sure why this is but many Danes have a really defensive attitude about it.

One American blogger, Roosh V, tells this story from his trip to Denmark:

It was common for a Danish girl to joke that Americans like cheeseburgers and French fries.

I would counter her observation with one of my own by saying, "We love hamburgers, but you guys like the kebabs. Those places are everywhere." Pretty innocuous comment, right? Wrong. The Danish girl gets offended and counters with, "No, Danish food culture is quite varied. You're not looking hard enough to find other places." Really, bitch? There would be no less than four kebab shacks within a stone's throw.

There are so many kebab shacks in Copenhagen that if an alien landed in Denmark he'd conclude that kebabs, shawarmas, and gyros have been Danish cuisine staples for thousands of years. I'd ask Danish people what their typical cuisine is and they'd give me an answer like "thick wheat bread with meat on it." In other words, sandwiches. Yeah, real indigenous. They'd rather die than admit that a "stupid American" got them pegged.

In my opinion, the best traditional Danish cuisine is still to be had in a Danish home where it is served with pride. It is here also that you may experience the illusive hygge (Danish coziness) which adds to the pleasure of the experience.

Regardless of who serves it, I have my own phobias with Danish cuisine. Now Danes, please don't get upset with me.

For example, there are millions of weird Danish lunch products that are beyond stinky. Strange smells, textures and shapes and I swear it feels foreign to touch it. And there are loads of funky fish products here that literally freak me out. Some of these include cooking the internal vital organs of fish that are nearly human size – boiling and eating them. This delicacy is affectionately called Torskerogn.

Cod roe comes packaged in surprisingly sturdy, semi-transparent bags, with a mesh of not particularly appetizing blood vessels under the surface. The proper *Viking* way of (over)cooking them is to simply drop them into boiling water and wait 20-30 min. They come out gray, hard and brittle, looking like the giant scrotum of a dead, waterlogged junkie.

Definitely something that could have been removed by the surgeons at Seattle Grace and landing in the medical waste bin.

Another bizarre sight at the fish shop is a sky high pile of shiny, golden petrified fish. Smoked with heads, eyes and tails, intact – the eater gets the joy of slicing and dissecting the fish before eating.

If you want a souvenir of your Scandinavian fish experiences, go to the grocery store and you will find rows and rows of toothpaste style tubes filled with mysterious fish spreads and pastes.

Leverpostej – a Danish Lunchtime Staple and national dish

I actually give myself a taste test twice every year of leverpostej (pork liver pate). Hoping that as I move closer to becoming a Dane, some miraculous change in taste will allow me to love this beloved lunchtime classic and national dish.

I honestly can say that that time has yet to come. Every few months or so, I put a small piece in my mouth and hope.

For the first few seconds, wait... maybe... Ok...

Ick.....now, here comes the murky aftertaste.

No. I still don't like it.

Spoon goes in the sink.

A variation of the leverpostej sandwich is something called the Veterinarian's Midnight Snack, which is pork liver pate, corned beef and 'sky' – a meat flavored brown gelatin. My guess for the name is that the concoction was made from all the dead animal parts leftover from the Vet's clinic.

But what does this have to do with happiness you ask?

According to "What You Eat can Affect Your Happiness!," by accredited practicing dietitian Sharon Natoli B vitamins have a role in regulating mood, energy and memory. Recent research indicates that folate, vitamin B6 and B12 may have particularly important roles in regulating various aspects of mood and thus happiness.

Her top Five Happy Foods – spinach, parsley, sunflower seeds, strawberries and beetroot are found in many Danish specialties.

Beetroot is found at nearly every lunch table, sunflower seeds are found in Danish rugbrød and muesli and fresh grown local strawberries are eaten by the million during the peak summer months. Oprah fell in love with rugbrød during her last visit and has arranged for it to be sent to her in Chicago.

In addition, all the funky fish products including the oily fish that is in Danish herring products have an omega fat called DHA (docohexanoic acid) that is required in high amounts as part of brain tissue. These tissues regulate mood and have been known to reduce depression.

So yes, to make a long story short, I think that Danish food is very nutritious but not very delicious and may make a very small contribution to the well-being of Danes – both physically and mentally. Funnily enough in the world's most unhappy place, Moldova, a depressing chunk of the former Soviet Union, the best thing that anyone could say about their homeland was that the vegetables and fruit were fresh.

On the other hand, I think Danish food has a long way to go before it becomes a mainstay in world cuisines and eating it may not make one happy – especially when you get your bill from Noma, at 1000 USD per head.

Activities represents those factors under your voluntary control.

To me Activities is the most important ingredient in the recipe. It is here where one can be really active in affecting one's happiness and take a leadership role in steering one's life towards happiness.

With regards to Danish happiness, I think that the Danes work towards this in their attitudes about community, values and beliefs which are influenced heavily by the Janteloven.

In addition, the Jante law supports activities that promote happiness in healthy ways by focusing on mindfulness, flow, pleasure and gratifications.

Janteloven

I don't believe that the only reason the Danes are happy is because they live in a heavy social welfare community with all the benefits such as universal healthcare, free education and unemployment tax (C). These are all good things but it does not make Denmark unique -- most European countries have similar types of programs. In addition, as I mentioned, the Danes don't have access to great weather or inexpensive and varied food stuffs either. So what is their secret?

Denmark's entire social welfare community has roots with a group dynamic that negatively portrays and criticizes individual success, materialism and achievement as worthless and unsuitable.

Observed as a form of behavior for centuries, it was identified as a series of unwritten rules, the Jante Law, by the Danish/Norwegian author Aksel Sandemose. In his fiction novel '*A Fugitive Crosses His Tracks*' in 1933, he portrays a small fictional Danish town called **Jante,** modeled on his own hometown of Nykøbing Mors as it was at the beginning of the 20th Century.

Many Danes that you speak to about the Jante law are a bit ashamed of it. Jante law is considered a snide, jealous and narrow-minded small-town mentality that refuses to acknowledge individual effort. Instead, it places all emphasis on the collective, while punishing those who stand out as achievers. On the surface, most Danish people admit that this is not a progressive, civilized way of thinking.

Talk to Danes about the Jante law and they start squirming in their seats...

"Yeees, we have the Jante law and it's terrible," they will say evasively. "But we can't really do anything about it."

I felt many times that conversations became really uncomfortable when talking about the J-law. Those I spoke to and asked about it would not admit that they put down other people's achievements. In reality, it seemed as if they were in some kind of a strange denial.

One older gentleman said well, yes, he could understand envy. For example, he envied my long wavy hair. It seemed that people were missing my point, indeed most Danes I interviewed admitted that they had never read the actual Jante law nor could they point out instances where it was prevalent.

There are ten different rules in the law as defined by Sandemose, but they are all variations on a single theme and are usually referred to as a homogeneous unit:

Don't think you're anyone special or that you're better than us!

The problem is I think Aksel Sandemose, like most fictional writers, exaggerated his points to create a work of fiction. We all know that many times, social laws or cultural norms are extremely subtle.

So subtle, many times you think it may just a temporary blemish, a figment of the imagination but no indeed, the Jante law is a real and living virus pulsating through Danish life.

Jante law exists in a moderate, more conventional way that explains daily life in Denmark. It spans everything from the tax system to how people decide to commute to work.

I think the Jante law has been given a bad rap. Talking to Danes about the positive sides of the Jante law is almost impossible. Danes get very confused, yes, they hear the arguments, interesting but...don't they ultimately hate the Jante law?

Is this a trick question, they wonder carefully as they speak with me. They can't admit to it. It is wrong to be against individualism, creativity, entrepreneurship, success... or is it?

I had my own 'personal' run-ins with the Jante law. Ostentation is frowned upon and the outward trappings of success – the luxury car or the bigger house -- met with strong disapproval and feelings of waste.

One Danish fitness instructor told me his Jante law story. One night, he and his friends were biking home from a nightclub at 2 am when they saw a Porsche veer off the road and into a ravine.

They rode by and saw that the driver was alive but when he rolled down the window, they gave him the finger and said with a mean laugh, 'You get what you deserve, rich prick.'

Most of my new Danish friends did not understand my strong desire for 'trading up' to a larger and flashy dream house. My friend Miss K said, "But, Sharmi, you only have one child and who wants to vacuum clean such a large house?"

For me, the bigger dream house represented 'arrival.' I had arrived at success and could show my glamorous and perfect life to the world-- my friends, family and more importantly others.

Even now, I sometimes have to explain why (or avoid the subject altogether) I don't bike the 15 kilometers to my office everyday instead of wastefully driving a car and polluting the earth.

To my astonishment, I also had trouble getting a job in Denmark. My first several interviews, the feedback was much unexpected. Managers I met with all said that although I had fantastic qualifications, they felt I had 'talked' too much about myself in their interviews. Apparently, I seemed overconfident and pretentious. They said I gave too many examples of my own achievements instead of speaking more modestly, and giving credit to others.

'Whaaat?' but this was a job interview for a managerial public relations position at an international pharmaceutical company, not a Geisha gig at a tea ceremony. In order to eventually get a job, I had to turn down the volume about myself significantly, gave credit to others who didn't deserve it and pretended to be more humble. I got the job and didn't have to wear a kimono.

On the flip side, my brother-in-law was so discreet that I sometimes felt he was hiding stuff just to play the modesty card. Like he was nominated for a CIO (Chief IT Officer) of the year award and the way his family and friends found out was by first reading about it in the papers.

Here are the ten rules of Jante :

Don't think that you are special.

Don't think that you are of the same standing as us.

Don't think that you are smarter than us.

Don't fancy yourself as being better than us.

Don't think that you know more than us.

Don't think that you are more important than us.

Don't think that you are good at anything.

Don't laugh at us.

Don't think that any one of us cares about you.

Don't think that you can teach us anything.

OK, these are pretty terrible and would lead most Americans to run the other way. But if carefully looked at the laws could be re-written in a PR friendly, spinned way. Indeed, similar to the way it is actually practiced in Denmark today.

Yes, Sandemose's original Jante law is harsh. But in Denmark, the unwritten and nearly unspoken actions behind Jante law are more subtle (therefore it is easy to step into them by accident and make a mess).

The idea is simply - Avoid Creating Envy in Others.

This is my interpretation of the **real-life** Jante Loven prevalent in Denmark today:

- If you are 'somebody special,' please be very discreet about it and let others tell us about your attributes.
- We are all very good in our own way.
- We are all smart in our own way.
- No one is better than anyone else (a high school dropout is as good as a PhD).
- If you are good at something, please be very discreet about it and let others tell us about your attributes.
- Understand our ways, blend in and become part of the 'samfund' – community.
- We have our own values and ways of thinking that creates a peaceful co-existence – change is not really welcome.
- Envy is the killer of happiness and therefore promotion of it – will be met with disinterest.

There are loads of examples where you experience this self-deprecating attitude in Denmark. Carlsberg is an internationally known Danish beer company and it is one of the most popular and well-known beers world-wide and yet its slogan is:

Probably the Best Lager in the World.

In Denmark, even if you are the best, (most will think you are not) you should be modest and discreet about it. There is no place for bragging and those who need to shout it from the roof tops never receive the audiences they are looking for.

Compare it to Budweiser's slogan – King of Beers,

The term 'braggart' (blærerov) or a windbag -- exhibiting self-importance/self-promotion -- is considered a bad trait and is frowned upon and maybe why Budweiser has low sales in Denmark. At the Danish workplace, the way to win the crowd is to have others promote and praise you.

Although Danish beer brand Carlsberg's tagline "Probably the best lager in the world" was created in 1973 by Saatchi and Saatchi, it has a distinct Danish feel to it. Again, the idea is not to tell others you are the best. If you are, let others make that decision for you.

If you are complimented about your beautiful home, you should say 'ikke så dårligt' – 'it's not so bad', in order to undervalue its worth. Never say, thank you, because that would mean you are appreciating the praise.

Janteloven is a Win-Win Game

It is better to want what you have than to have what you want

For decades, economists have stressed the contradiction between high ambition and the stagnation of happiness in high-income countries. The creators of the Jante law realized that rising aspirations created by the desperate search for status would be detrimental to their collective community.

Why play the game? The creators of Jante Law changed the rules by encouraging modesty and reducing envy by squashing individual ambition. They knew that individual success and prosperity was a zero sum game.

In order to win in normal competitions, others have to lose. But why should anyone value such as system? Why not create a system with different values? Values that are not based on material things. Values based on collective success and a win-win attitude. Values like the Danish system.

Similar to the experience of the young man in Sandemose's book who moved to the fictional small town in Denmark, I found that coming from one of the largest superpowers in the world provided me with no credibility here.

My money was useless, (the dollar is worth nothing outside of USA), my attitude was too American and ? (not a good thing). For my part, I thought Denmark should change – adopt a better work ethic (work longer and therefore harder?), keep shops open ALWAYS! And while I was at it, why weren't people impressed with what I do?

If I was here to foist my American ideals on the Danes, the attitude seemed to be I could just forget about it, pack my Louis Vuitton suitcase and get on the next SAS flight out of here.

The Jante laws are here to preserve idyllic, happy communal living standards in Denmark. While at first it seemed hard to grasp (forget about me and all my material desires!), the Jante law promised me more – a new economy that was not based on money and wealth, but based on satisfaction.

The successful person under the Jante law was not rich but was happy because they belonged to a community that supported better values and ways of thinking that resulted in happiness for everyone.

Unpeeling the Happiness Onion

<u>Janteloven Goes Across Everything and Everyone</u>

Occasionally I am invited as a guest lecturer for a course on positive psychology at the University of Copenhagen. I created the Janteloven onion model to explain my perspectives:

Janteloven Onion

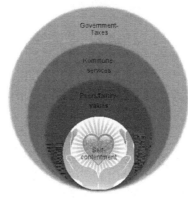

A mentality that underpins the egalitarian Danish tax system, the social welfare society and the everyday contentment that Danes have.

The Jante Law places everyone on an equal footing: in Denmark, a doctor is no better than a garbage man. These equalities lead to a very satisfied existence here, where everyone has similar levels of self-esteem, feelings of success, and overall contentment with life.

Funnily enough, those two even make the same salary. For example, a doctor at a public hospital makes less than $70,000/year (starting wages) and a garbage collector—or, to use the politically-correct term, "Sanitation Technician"—also earns $70,000 on average. In Denmark, the income for the 10% richest is only five times higher than the 10% at the other end of the scale, whereas in the USA the difference is 16 times higher.

While Danes have a desire to become successful, their definition of success might be more realistic and less extravagant than the definition Americans might have. In Denmark, American tendencies of always wanting more, thinking BIG or believing the grass is greener on the other side could be counterproductive. At least they were for me.

While American sayings like "be the brightest star in the sky" encourage individuals to strive above the rest, the Jante law discourages judgment and belittling of people who chose to live in a more simple and humble way, making 'everyone a star'.

The previous chapters outline some of the most significant research in happiness and subjective well-being. The evidence says that more money does not make people happier.

Outer Layer: Positive Attitudes Towards Welfare State

In Denmark, the systems/structures put in place, such as the massive tax system, discourage personal gain by placing a very high price on those 'tall poppies' – people with great wealth – to make sure that everyone has the baseline and therefore the same possibilities for happiness.

Here, the Danish system spreads wealth and provides universal healthcare, public education, and unemployment insurance to all. The beauty of the Jante law is that it supports this system by also keeping personal norms and behaviors in-check by encouraging a culture that values modesty, moderation and community. The system is called 'samfund' and although the English translation is society – I propose that the real meaning is 'same fund' and that Danes all live from the one pot of money.

What I find amazing is the personal strengths of Danes; in the US people want less government intervention and want to contribute as little as possible to the greater good, here it is the opposite.

Most people in Denmark, which boasts some of the world's highest taxes, believe their tax rate is appropriate. More than one in 10 think they don't pay enough. The Greens Analyseinstitut survey, published in the financial daily Boersen, indicated that a full 66 percent of Danes agree with their level of taxation, while only 20 percent think taxes are too high.

Many Danes are satisfied that they are getting their money's worth –that is, they enjoy tangible benefits from the taxes they pay in terms of universal health care, tuition-free education through to the university level, and employment benefits and security. More importantly, they feel good about the system and everyone wants to contribute. Although numerous political parties have tried to reduce taxes and thereby cut down on the 'samfund' – these efforts have been futile.

Ironically, the Danish word for tax 'skat' is also the word for 'honey/sweetheart' – I can't imagine anyone in the US calling their darling 'income tax' or 'capital gains tax'. But skat in Denmark represents a positive, important force – it ensures that everyone has enough money to cover their basic needs, understanding that more money loses its positive effect.

Middle Layer: Community and Peers

What exactly makes up a strong community under the Jantloven? A community that supports and nourishes ideals such a classlessness, sameness and free access for all – this provides a safe, positive and supportive place for all members to thrive.

One of the most important factors towards happiness and well-being in Denmark is gender equality both in the workplace and at home, through the systems put in place. The Janteloven creates a situation where 'everyone' is the same; both men and women. There is full equality here for both men and women and that goes across everything from the studies you choose, to the job you take, to who makes the Danish meatballs and takes the kids to football practice.

Denmark boasts an impressive record on gender equality, ranking 7th in the 2008 Global Gender Gap Report conducted by the World Economic Forum.

A journalist from the Washington Post, who was writing a book about stressed and overwhelmed working mothers, visited me in Denmark awhile back. She asked about life in Denmark and she and I chatted and concluded that, yes, it was indeed nice to be in Denmark as a working mother.

Danish women have a lot to smile about as the systems and attitudes both within the community and through the state provide support and incentives for them to have a happy and fulfilling career and family life. Danish women have one of the highest employment rates among women in Europe and OECD countries at 70.8% percent.

For example, local funding supports childcare fully. Daycare is high quality, safe and practically free, plus nearly all kids attend from age six months and upwards and love it. In addition, for those few housewives who stay at home and take care of their own child, the state sends them a paycheck too.

By law, women are allowed to take one year paid maternity leave and spend it with their newborn children at home. Plus, Danish employers are required to keep their jobs waiting for them for when they return.

Mild and good humored, Danish men are egalitarian and have no problems doing laundry, caring for children and cooking in addition to working fulltime. They are in touch with their feminine side and recent statistics show an increase in the number of men going on paternity leave to take care of the kids, while their highly educated and ambitious wives are working.

The work/life balance is something that is often talked about at annual reviews with supervisors and it is important as a manager in Denmark that you talk about this balance with your employees.

And the Danish 37.5 hour work week. Yes, it is true, most Danish men and women seriously come into the office at 8 a.m. in the morning and leave at 4 p.m. SHARP. This means they have time for sports, leisure and their families and have a true balance of work and home life.

Danes Have Fewer Friends but Tighter Networks

As I have mentioned earlier, Denmark has been criticized as being one of the most foreigner-unfriendly countries in the world and a quick visit to a Copenhagen shop or restaurant supports this point fully. Funnily enough this maybe one of the reasons they are also the most happy.

Recent studies on expatriates in Denmark by the Oxford research group reveal that 71 per cent of the foreigners who believed they would stay more than three years, did not stay (many actually left earlier). And the study showed that Danes' unfriendliness and lack of welcoming behavior was an important factor in them leaving.

The thing is many Danes stick to a small network of close friends and family. It is not uncommon to not have more than 5-8 families that Danes see on a regular basis.

I was actually told courteously by one Danish woman when she turned down my dinner invitation, 'I am sorry but we have enough friends.'

As you know, I straddle two worlds – my American heritage, friends, family and expats and the Danish culture that I have now become a part of through my husband and daughter and our Danish friends and family.

The reserved nature of the Danes takes some getting used to. I have experienced the most extreme example of how cultural friendliness differs from country to country.

During a spinning class that I took while on a business trip in Chicago: I arrived ten minutes early and by the end of the class, everyone in the class including the instructor knew my name, how long I was staying, where I was from and whether I enjoyed living in Denmark.

I have been going to the same gym and spinning class in my Danish neighborhood for about six years and no one knows my name! Even more ludicrous, I attended a girl's night dinner party and was sitting next to the instructor of my spinning class. I casually mentioned that I really liked her class the day before and she looked at me puzzled, like who are you?

I thought my head was going to explode ... 'How many Indian looking women take your spin class every week and are in the front row?!!'

Let's just say that the Danes are a reticent bunch and even when I had wowed them with my fantastic, heavily accented Danish, it took years of hard work to make them friends. It is not unusual to have close colleagues at the office for years but never be invited to any personal engagements. Entertaining at home is not relevant in a business context.

When meeting a Dane, they are pleasant and informal but difficult to get to know. Not just with foreigners but also with themselves as well. An invitation to their private home is unusual so if you get one, take it.

Inspired by Sartre's No Exit, my X father-in-law used to say, 'one should never become friends with the neighbors because if you have a dispute or a disagreement about something, you will be stuck living next to them and that hell is worse than any potential friendship.'

Okkkay. But I was unwilling to listen and pushed ahead with my plans to conquer the neighborhood with some good old American hospitality. I believed that gracious hospitality, gourmet cooking and a generous spirit would melt the hearts of the Danes.

My first winter in Denmark in my new home with Mr. X, I invited all the neighbors for a Christmas Open house party.

In retrospect, I now know that that was a 'no-no' – Christmas (ALL of December) is a sacred time reserved for one's selected family and friends. It is not a time when you want to congregate with strangers...So, you guessed it, only one couple came to my party.

Unfortunately, my zealousness scared off the other Danish neighbors permanently (who began to think of me as an over-friendly, inappropriate and possibly annoying pest), I was ostracized and I never got to know any of them. They quickly moved to the other side of the street, jumped behind hedges whenever I passed by or they pretended not to see me at all.

One of my best Danish girlfriends now, I had invited to my home with her husband for fabulous home cooked dinners for two years straight before I received an invitation back to her place. But I was determined to win her over and now ten years later, I am considered a close friend (but still cannot be compared to friends she has had for over 20 years....)

Another one of my good friends is originally from England, we will call her Miss M. After more than 15 years in Denmark, she has not learned her lessons about Danes and how to cultivate friendships. She still sadly anticipates a return invitation each time she hosts someone. I encourage her to keep trying but alas she gives up quickly thinking another Dane will be different.

But Danes do not feel obligated to return a dinner invitation. They normally have brought you a hostess gift and sent you a text message or Facebook message the day after with a Tak for sidst (thanks for last night). Then they will disappear into oblivion until you invite them again.

Danes are culturally reserved so breaking through the friendship barrier takes hard work and determination but the rewards are great.

Once you have a Danish friend, you have a friend for life. If you have a problem, they will come to your rescue and will be there for you in thick and thin. They can be the warmest and kindest people you know....giving and helpful.

Studies also support the Danish attitude towards friendships. While having a few friends may not make you a winner on Facebook, a small, devoted core of friends — between two and four — appears to provide the greatest payoff in terms of stability, happiness and coping.

I had always focused on a larger but shallower social net, but found in my times of need a handful of good friends was all I needed.

Most Danes are respectful of other people's personal space and therefore rarely make the first move and this has given them the 'unfriendly' label. But younger generation Danes have taken this to heart and there are a few movements going on to change this nationwide cultural outlook.

I was having a coffee with some Danish friends when one of my buddies mentioned that I should start following the Fucking Flink (FFlink) movement. In Danish, flink means 'polite' so it seemed a bit out there with the F-word but I guess the aggressive language is meant to catch your attention. It certainly caught mine.

The FFlink movement was started by a Danish advertising guy, Lars AP who was painfully made aware of the paradox that while Danes are the happiest people in the world, they are also some of the least friendly.

Why are they perceived as not so friendly? Because they are too polite (fucking flink!), he says.

Danes obsessed with not intruding in other people's business, determined to mind their own affairs and mindful of your personal space end up seeming cold and reserved. But too much personal space and well... people end up isolated and lonely including the Danes.

He wanted to make a change in this national behavior so he wrote a book (Fucking Flink) and he took to the streets to change his own behavior along with his friends and family. Now he and his followers do good deeds and then post the evidence/stories on Facebook. According to his research, not only do 'do-gooders' experience elevated levels of joy, the people around them who witnessed the 'act' do as well.

WOW, I love the concept and I totally commend this guy for trying to make changes in a culture so seemingly set in its way. In an interview he mentioned that he wanted these friendly 'acts' to be genuine and that cranking up the social thermometer would allow Danes to be playful with each other and shape informal bonds of friendship. Maybe this could spread to friendliness to foreigners too? How about befriend your expat neighbor and invite them for a cup of tea?

I must confess that my earlier attempts of random acts of kindness have fallen flat in Denmark (most of these transpire in the grocery store – sorry, I don't take public transport). For example, there was the time, when I tried to lend a hand to an elderly gentlemen with packing his groceries – (I think he thought I was trying to steal from him) – because he was very alarmed and asked me to 'back off'. In another instance, a haphazard fellow in front of me toppled all his groceries while standing in the check-out line. I tried to help him, but instead he asked me to leave him alone, and skip ahead of him.

These instances, stick out in my mind because it is actually worse to be rebuffed than to not do the deed at all....(at least that is how it felt at the time).

The Danes also need to ALLOW that people 'enter' their personal space and give them gifts of kindness and help...not to be suspicious of 'strangers' but be open and curious about others.

I am really excited about this movement and I hope to be soon posting some of my good deeds online if someone will let me make one □! I have a dream of being able to prevent someone from getting a nasty parking ticket by quickly buying some time on a parking meter.

Danish Bicycle Community

I have a confession: I can't ride a bike properly. In Denmark this is almost a crime, since in Copenhagen, one person in three commutes by bike to work or school every day and there are more bicycles than people in Denmark.

To be very precise about this statement, I can ride once the wheels are turning and when I am in balance and moving...it's the stopping and starting that I am seriously terrible at. It's so bad that I ask my daughter not to bike too close to me in case I happen to tip over and crush her by accident.

This is, of course, linked to my lazy parents who never removed the training wheels from my first bike.

In my defense for this crime (and my other crime of being a driver of a car in Denmark), I have to say that in the U.S., we do not have a bicycle culture. Many kids do not ride bikes, there are few to no bike paths in most neighborhoods and we are happy if we have a sidewalk we can walk on. Of course, drivers that whizz by give walkers a quick look of pity since people who walk are normally considered homeless.

On the other hand, Danes are active cyclists, often using their bikes to commute to work or to go off on trips at the weekend. And cycling is generally perceived as a healthy, environmentally friendly, cheaper and often quicker way around town than public transport or car. It is municipal policy for the number of people who commute by bike to go up to 40% by 2012 and 50% by 2015 in Copenhagen.

OK, but what does this have to do with the Laws of Jante and Danish Happiness?

I have a suspicion that the Danish cycling culture may have a double whammy effect - cycling and exercise in general promotes good health and happiness - and as a nice side effect they help to reduce envy (most people don't consider their bicycle as a status symbol) and promote equality as nearly everyone (besides me) can ride a bike.

While we all know this is the case, I think what is most interesting is the way that the Danish systems support this.

Being a car owner is like being a cross between vermin and a dairy cow. It's really not cool to drive and it comes with a huge tax burden with nearly 200 percent taxes on the car itself, road tax and gas tax.

Compare that to my cycling friends who are blessed with a tiny sales tax on the bike, no extra bike path tax and of course, no gas tax!

There has been some research on the link between sports participation, exercise and happiness. For example, experiments comparing American and Italian teens showed that people tended to be happiest when engaging in sports and games.[vi]

Danes support this premise wholeheartedly and try to make sure that their life is just a bike able (?). For example, Danes choose jobs, schools and even the homes they purchase that are bike-able distances from each other. One Dane said to me , 'my greatest happiness in life is that I can bike to work every morning.'

I have thought long and hard about the differences between Danes and Americans and how this attitude is so different.

Again, it is here that perhaps the Laws of Jante work again. The Laws of Jante say 'Don't fancy yourself as being better than us' – i.e. don't park your Ferrari here!

Inner onion- The Danish SELF

The Janteloven takes an important step in making sure that Danes focus on positive emotions including gratitude, satisfaction, contentment, optimism, realistic hopes and trust. While the systems from the government provide a great life for the whole community – it is you the individual that must focus on the rest – your personal happiness.

This is why I believe that the divorce rate in Denmark is so high, there is a great focus on the personal right to happiness and making sure you wake up every day with someone who makes your heart skip a beat. But it goes far beyond choosing a new partner - a tiny spring flower, a great kiss, a chocolate cupcake from Magnolia bakery, even finding a dime – all of these can make us happy in a transitory way. And these types of experiences in our day-to-day living can make a difference when questioned about our life satisfaction.

An ingenious experiment conducted by researcher Norbert Schwarz demonstrates the importance of transitory 'happiness' on reported life satisfaction with a group of Americans.

Before these people turned in the satisfaction questionnaire, Dr. Schwarz asked them to make a photocopy of the questionnaire. For half of the subjects, a dime was planted on the copy machine.

Reported life satisfaction was a point higher for those who found a dime! In other words, people rated their overall life happiness better based on something that happened five minutes ago.

This reminds me of the time my new Danish husband once pointed to some tiny yellow and white blossoms popping out of the snow on a winter's day.

'Look,' he said pointing to these really tiny weed-looking flowers, 'how beautiful, the vintergækker flowers are out , Spring is on its way.'

He smiled.

'Huh,' said I, wondering where these gorgeous flowers were, 'All I see is snow and some weeds popping out.'

He shook his head. 'Look at these,' he pointed again to the weed-like flowers, growing out of the grass.

And then suddenly I did see them – hundreds of them. Yes, on closer look these tiny flowers were very intricate – they had teeny blue green leaves and white, teardrop-shaped flowers. In fact they were quite beautiful and yet since I probably would have overlooked them for a large cultivated rose, I would have missed them.

It just goes to show the power of these smaller bites of happiness – and again it seems to me that the Danes had this one all figured out.

Like OMG. It's HYGGE

One of the most fundamental aspects of Danish culture is a concept called "Hygge', pronounced *HueGaah*.

It is a word you will hear endlessly here in Denmark and to describe many things – a moody candlelit table, an intimate dinner party, a warm silky bath, a delicious gourmet coffee, a freshly baked cake straight from the oven, even watching TV with the family. And with regards to Christmas – it could include decorating your home for Christmas, folding paper tree decorations with your children, drinking warm glogg (mulled wine) and of course eating the traditional Danish Christmas dinner with roast duck, caramel potatoes, red cabbage and baked apples.

In Denmark, hygge allows for conviviality to balance out consumerism and all the Christmas materialism we experience in other cultures like in the States.

Danes try to experience hygge on a daily/weekly basis, but as you can imagine they go into full overdrive during Christmas. It is rumored that hygge evolved from necessity because of the cold and dark Scandinavian winters. People would huddle together in small rooms around the fire and drink warm alcoholic drinks.

Instead of huddling around the fire, it is now the large living room TV with a bowl of Guf (candy, chips or maybe homemade goodies). I recently read an article that Danish television is playing a larger part of modern hygge by creating shows that the whole family wants to watch together – X Factor, Talent, Bingo Banko and the Danish version of Dancing with the Stars (Vild med Dans).

Hygge, loosely translated can be considered "coziness" and includes the presence of and pleasure from comforting, gentle, and soothing things. Hygge is described as a deep sense of place; well-being; a feeling of friendship, warmth, contentment and peace with your immediate surroundings.

The true essence of hygge is lost if it is too elegant, too extravagant, too luxurious. Hygge must be modest in a way, mundane and familiar – it is the celebration of the dull that hygge embodies.

Indeed the Danish author Hartmann Petersen mused that hygge had Freudian like tendencies – reflecting back to the womb. Therefore warmth and enclosure are essential elements of hygge.

What's great about hygge is that it is easy to come by. What's so special about it - Danes are able to recognize it, label it and appreciate it.

Funnily when I reflect on hygge and hyggeligt things, they are not necessarily Danish – lighting of candles, huddling with a blanket, intimate times with friends and family, fresh baked bread, a family TV night – we have all experienced it. The difference is that Danes prioritize it.

When you read the literature on happiness, or what researchers call Subjective Well Being (SWB), they roughly split happiness into two areas - in the moment happiness (like finding the dime!) and a longer term contentment.

I hypothesize that Danes actually work on both. The Laws of Jante provide a longer term contentment by creating focus on community, sameness, equality and reduced materialism (exceptions include Danish design lamps). On the other hand, hygge gives us the daily joys and pleasures needed for day-to-day well-being and happiness.

Remember the study I mentioned earlier, reported life satisfaction was higher for those people who found a dime, like 5 minutes ago.

Well, hygge can symbolically be the dime – small moments of happiness. My Danish X husband once said to me 'life should be a string of small happy moments.'

I guess I was not providing these daily happy moments -- hence the X -- but nonetheless like pearls on a string, can Danish hygge moments lead to a life time of happiness? I needed to know.

I therefore made a self-experiment. In the spirit of Fraulein Maria from the "Sound of Music," I made a list of my favorite everyday things -- white tea roses, Molton Brown liquid soap, Irish soda bread, interior design books, vampire paperbacks, all Diane Keaton movies, sparkly lipgloss, teen soap operas (yes I like Gossip Girl), Diet Coke -- and vowed to incorporate these in my life for six weeks. In addition, I threw in some standard 'hygge' necessities – loads of candles, firewood and my duvet.

At first, my family was suspicious and noted that I was acting peculiar and a bit odd. My daughter asked me if I was sick when I was wrapped in my duvet, sipping a warm cup of tea and gazing at the snow falling. When I replied that I was experimenting with Hygge Sig (self-inflicted coziness). She raised her eyebrows and flashed me a doubtful look. Did she think I was trying too hard? Was I doing it wrong? Hanging around, lounging on the sofa was not normal behavior for me...on the other hand, besides the growing stress of feeling like a couch potato, it did feel nice and relaxing.

I was indeed enjoying the sweetness of doing nothing or what the Italians call 'Il Dolce Far Niente.' Between you and me, it sounds far more glamorous than what my American girlfriends describe as 'vegging out.'

I interviewed a Danish anthropologist Jeppe Trolle Linnet who has done his PhD on hygge and considers himself to be a hygge expert.

'In Denmark, we just have sense of hygge. We say goodbye with "kan du hygge dig!" ("you can enjoy yourself!") or the classic statement "hvor var det bare hyggeligt" "wow, that was just nice and cozy." It is not necessary to explain more - hygge is in everyone's lives,' said Jeppe. He is an anthropologist and consumer researcher at the Institute of Marketing and Management, University of Southern Denmark.

A hygge event or gathering is characterized by social proximity - you are together, but it should not be too intense or fantastic. The idea is not to have great debates, gregarious discussions or even a frank talk about the inner truths of each other. Hygge has a light and humorous tone, says Jeppe Trolle Linnet.

Hygge often takes place in the home, but can also be with friends or at a restaurant. A cozy place will often be shielded from the outside world, there will be soft furnishings and perhaps a living fire, which is one of the very best ways to create cosiness.

 People often sit and eat some snacks when they are having fun, but it must be something simple, like homemade. When you have fun, it's not about sophisticated table settings or to dupe people and entertain them in a luxury like manner, says Jeppe Trolle Linnet.

Something really interesting, he said, is that Danes really enjoy themselves and enjoy hygge when everyone contributes including the children, and no one is allowed to dominate the conversation.

The truth is that I can see what he is talking about. When hygge is really apparent– there is some kind of similarity between everyone who is present and everyone works to preserve the equality – keeping conversation, light, polite, entertaining, hyggeligt – no-one's emotions should be peaking.

'It's something we Danes have learned, a kind of bodily knowledge that we use when we are together without being able to put it into words. Foreigners often have difficulty with it, he says.'

Yes, I think sarcastically to myself. 'Hygge is a national sport in Denmark.'

Jeppe Trolle Linnet is often asked if hygge is really something especially Danish. And the answer is no. You can enjoy it in other countries. But what makes it special, is that there is no other country where coziness is elevated to a national treasure and how it is linked to pure Danish-ness, he says.

He claims that the Danish bourgeoisie created and introduced the concept of Hygge in the 1800s, and they regarded themselves as the most 'hyggeligt' Danes.

The idea stems from a rejection of the upper class, where social manners were stiff and where the father and other men were the central figure and dominated the conversation.

In addition, he says that hygge was also excluded in the lower social strata where the children, for example in the countryside, were sent out to the fields to work and the family unit worked hard just to survive.

These days hygge is a result of the political culture war in Denmark and hygge could be seen as core values of the traditional socialist.

'Funny enough, a more open attitude to things might seem to be more anti hygge, he says.

Hygge plays a very important role in life here in Denmark. While having cozy experience in the U.S. occurs in a happenstance way, I believe Danes truly embrace it and prioritize it. I can understand it because once you incorporate hygge into your life then you want to keep it going. When you read the literature on happiness, it talks about happiness in the moment and a more longer term contentment.

I hypothesize that Danes actually work on both. The Laws of Jante provide a longer term contentment by creating focus on community, sameness, equality and reduced materialism – on the other hand hygge gives us the daily joys and pleasures needed for well-being.

Who Cares What You Do for a Living, Tell Me about Your Sports and Hobbies

In the US, the typical question after you are introduced to someone at a party is 'what do you do?' but here it is 'what sports do you do?' This is quite a safe topic since thanks to the Danish social welfare system, there are a lot of people 'who don't do anything' and most think that a job/career is not a reflection of themselves.

This is so different compared to my friends and family in the U.S. All my American friends were striving to be Vice Presidents by 30 and their 'fancy' business cards were given out as often as handshakes. In Denmark, I have never, ever received a business card from someone at a party or a social engagement.

I think the Jante law supports this, the barriers for entry with regards to sports is low - so everyone has access.

Regardless, the sports topic is endless, at any dinner party, airport or café, you can always find Danes talking about their sports/exercise/routines. They swim, play handball, softball, mountain bike, cycle, sail, play tennis, badminton, ice hockey, and golf and they do it well.

No surprise, almost two million Danes actively engage in association sports and sports clubs, corresponding to about 40% of the Danish population.

Danes have work-life balance. Which means *fritids interesse* (free time interests) is an important word here. The average Dane pursues it with vigor. I have never known so many different types of sports, cultural or artistic pursuits (all of which are subsidized by local government). You can learn to make rustic wild flower bouquets, take underwater judo lessons, participate in Roman history re-enactment camps for adults – all accessible and reasonably priced.

If you played soccer as a boy and loved it, why stop when you are pushing 50? Your local club offers Old Boys soccer. My Danish husband plays Veterans handball. The way he describes their games is farcical. These older gentlemen play rough every Monday night for about an hour until one falls over injured and then they all go out for a victory beer.

But since many people would never, ever talk about their work....

Danes will however speak to you nonstop about their personal sports and their exercising – 'I had the best run, blah, blah' – 'I cycled 30 kilometers in the wind, hail and rain and loved it, blah, blah blah'.

For me, exercising is just a form of daily grooming – something you must do in order for your body not to fall apart. It's like eating healthy, washing your face or brushing your teeth. I could just imagine telling my colleagues about the fantastic and very long teeth brushing I did that morning : You know I really got down deep into my molars with my electric toothbrush, gave myself a gum massage to top it off in warm salt water. It felt sooo good.'

But all joking aside, I had to admit that when you read the literature on happiness, happiness-in-the-present plays a large role in long term happiness /contentedness.

There are 2 types of happiness activities – Pleasures and Flow.

Pleasures are quick satisfactions of biological needs (like eating that soft serve ice cream), but the concept of flow means one should seek activities that achieve a unique state of mind, where time stops, where one is engaged and perhaps building psychological capital for the future.

Increasing the number of *flow* activities under your V (voluntary activities) in the happiness formula will tip your happiness scales and have little to do with money – making or spending it.

When you speak to a Dane, most will passionately tell you about their sports or leisure activities or hygge. The fact is that most of these activities give them flow – the daily joys and psychological pleasures needed for daily wellbeing and happiness

When it came to Danish 'flow' activities - the 'group party walk' springs to mind. One cold winter, I attended a semi-formal baby christening party in the nearby deer park in Klampenborg.

It is pretty windy and cold here in January, and I was looking forward to warming my legs at the open fireplace at the restaurant after the church ceremony when the hostess declared that we would all be taking a 'group walk' in the forest before the welcome drinks. Now I was wearing a short dress, pantyhose and a pair of Christian Louboutin high heeled pumps...ERRGG.

I was secretly beginning to panic when the ever trusty DH (Danish husband), reminded me that he brought my hiking boots in the car (just in case). Nearly all 50 guests put on their coats and we walked out together for a refreshing one hour tour in the natural surroundings.

Even after all these years, I just never know when a serendipitous 'walk' will creep up behind me, take me by surprise and I end up somewhere in the forest, beach, countryside, sandpit, lake, without a proper coat or footwear. And the days when the wind is blisteringly cold, I think a full face ski mask should also be added to the survival kit.

I will never forget the spur of the moment canoe trip that ended a picnic, one Danish summer. I ruined a pair of gorgeous sandals because the bank that our canoe drifted on to was actually quick mud and the moment I left the boat, I sank knee deep into the ground.

The other day I stumbled upon a quote about walking from the Danish philosopher Søren Kierkegaard : "Above all, do not lose your desire to walk: every day I walk myself into a state of well-being and walk away from every illness; I have walked myself into my best thoughts, and I know of no thought so burdensome that one cannot walk away from it...".

Walking was not part of my American culture. Many neighborhoods do not have sidewalks. In the US, we have our own indoor phenomenon called 'shopping mall walks' (seriously strange) and a walk in the forest is called a 'hike' and usually not done in party shoes....

That said, it is probably one of my favorite customs in Denmark and it has really changed my point of view about the simple pleasures of walking. It is actually a great way of socializing with friends and many of my Danish buddies and I meet in the forest, take a walk/chat, spot a few deer, perhaps grab a café latte – all year round.

Studies show that mood is also increased when people are surrounded by wilderness or beauty. In Denmark, the climate is fairly cold and cloudy but most Danes have access to forests, parks and wilderness.

Next fall, I plan to do a bit of mushroom hunting during a walk with my in-laws and they promise to make sure I don't die by eating poisonous fungi. (By the way, this is very necessary, since apparently the really delicious looking ones are fatal.)

I think it is the importance of fresh air, light exercise, taking in the outdoors and even experiencing different seasons that makes walking an important element contributing to Danish happiness. According to research in the journal *Environmental Health and Technology*, exercising in natural areas is not only good for your physical health—it can improve your mood and sense of well-being.

I encourage you to try it...yes, even in the freezing rain – take your ski mask! As the Danes say, it is not about the bad weather – it is about the right clothes for the weather.

According to Happiness experts some of the most important things that we can do to increase happiness in our lives is to focus on gratifications and 'flow' activities that enrich our lives.

There is also significant literature about physical activity, endorphins and a positive effect on mental wellbeing. It is well established that exercise improves mental well-being through improved mood and self-perception and is an effective treatment for clinical depression and anxiety.

As a 'New' Dane, I now take early morning walks on the tiny beach near our home. It is so nice to have a breath of fresh air before starting a hectic task-filled day inside the office.

A Great Obstacle To Happiness Is To Anticipate Too Great A Happiness.
Fontenelle, Du Bonheur (1687)

In addition to the numerous **activities** that Danes do to find flow, pleasures and gratifications they also have very different mindsets compared to the average American.

I've noticed that Danes manage their expectations and very few have ' dreams' for their futures. Many Danes focus on the pleasures of today and now, instead of thinking and dreaming about an uncertain tomorrow. They are 'tilfreds' or content with their lives and this gives them peace and comfort.

Ask a Dane about their dreams for the future – it sure is not about amassing great wealth, dying rich or becoming famous. When pushed, the Danish dream is about healthy lifestyle, family and comfortable circumstances.

In Kaare Christensen's article, '*Why are Danes Smug: comparative study of life satisfaction in the European union,*' he writes that Danes have the lowest expectations in the European Union, ranking among the bottom half.

He writes that it is plausible that unrealistic expectations could be the basis of disappointment and low life satisfaction. And therefore the opposite could be the case – instead of don't worry, be happy, it's don't expect anything good, be happy.

"What we basically figured out is that although the Danes were very happy with their life, when we looked at their expectations they were pretty modest," he says. When one has low expectations, one is rarely disappointed, he concluded.

Unfortunately, little research has been done on the concept that an entire population with low expectations can indeed lead to societal contentment and happiness.

Expecting the worst or having low expectations is a technique called bracing which has been studied by psychologists. Dr. James Shepperd, a psychology professor at the University of Florida published an article in the *Journal of Personality and Social Psychology* in which he studied the effects of bad financial news on needy students. While his study solely focused on financial need, it established a trait for investigating the effect of need on predictions for the future.

According to Shepperd, setting low expectations is a protective behavior. In fact, a bad outcome can actually feel good if you expected something worse. He concludes, "After all having high expectations and then being disappointed may make the hunger pains worse."

In similar research by Sylvia Perry, Perry found that certain kinds of persons, specifically, people with high defensive pessimism (a coping style characterized by ruminating on worse case scenarios when under stress), perform better under high academic pressure. Her study focused on pessimistic female students taking math tests under challenging conditions. When pessimists were faced with a challenging task they set low expectations for their performance even if the expectations were unrealistic.

She calls this effect 'Making Lemonade,' in which defensive pessimists (having lemons) use negative thinking as a defense mechanism in stressful situations to achieve positive outcomes.

In both studies, the persons who used these techniques, whether it was the financially needy students or pessimistic female math test takers, one thing was clear that low expectations or expecting the worse can lead to positive outcomes or feelings.

Danes have consistently low and (undoubtedly realistic) expectations for the years to come too, and yet were the happiest people in the world.

Is Denmark a country full of defensive pessimists? Hard to say.

Anthropologists have noted that the general environment, such as climate and geological features, can also shape a culture and explain certain personality traits typical in a given culture. Societies that have limited resources probably have had a history of making the best out of the resources they could gather.

For example, if a country has a climate that is very hot and dry, the society probably has an ability to save and conserve water very well. These learned behaviors can manifest themselves in personality traits for an entire society of people.

The fact that Denmark historically had lost most of its landmass in wars, boasted no real geological wonders of the worlds and has a soccer team that had never won the World cup could be related to an entire society of people with lowered expectations?

But wouldn't low expectations on a national level, where everyone believes they are not good at anything, breed a bunch of depressed losers?

This is not the case, as this book shows. It is indeed possible to achieve success without an ambitious, competitive spirit. Be good, be great but be humble and modest about it. Don't think, just act greatly and do your best because quality is important. Is it necessary to have winners if it means that there will also losers?

A story comes to mind of an American friend of my daughter who had a birthday party. Of course, there were party games and instead of sore losers, there were some sore winners. The Danish winning children were outraged that there were no 'trøste gave,' consolation prizes for the ones who lost. (In English we call this is a 'booby' prize and it is quite negative since it stems from the Spanish word *bobo* which means stupid).

Indeed, the ones most upset were the winners. These Danish children were almost embarrassed for winning and wanted to somehow share their prize with the group.

It was not fun to be a winner because it meant that their friends were losers, they said. Their friends didn't get candy and their friends had to feel the pain of envy. It was almost being punched twice for the losers – first they lost the game and then they didn't get a prize.

It is this interesting and communal way of thinking that pervades the school system and the way Danish children grow up. In Danish business school, I learned about a concept called **Win Win**, isn't it possible for everyone to win? Why do we need to have losers?

Danes believe everyone is important and valuable. Therefore it is really difficult to stand-out and become part of an elite because the 'elite' does not exist.

Even though there are a few private schools nearly all are heavily funded by the State and the tuition fees are nominal. There are no 'private' universities or colleges and you can't find one gated community if Denmark. If you are lucky enough to own beach property – strangers are even allowed to walk on it!

This way of thinking allows everyone access by removing all barriers and it emphasizes the importance of co-operation, sharing, caring and the success of the overall group versus domination, gate keeping, egotistical behavior and personal gain.

Because most Danish organizations and companies are flat structured (very few managers) and team based, much of Danish work seems to fit the bill for a win-win:

> Danes believe that
> 1. There are no losers (everyone contributes).
> 2. Everyone is involved (no-one is left out or forced out).
> 3. Win-Win works on many psychological levels (communicating openly, supporting each other, having fun in a group, removing authority figures, etc.)

This feeling of equality is felt everywhere. In Denmark, it is rare to ever use anyone's last name when addressing them. You even call your doctor by his first name 'Bent, Bo or Carsten' and never with a 'Dr.' in front of it. At my daughter's school, it always surprises me that she addresses her teachers with his/her first name rather than Mr./Mrs. Again this is to break down authority figures and level the playing field to give everyone the same rights. Even addressing the Prime Minister – a journalist would call her by first name in a press conference and not Mrs. Prime Minister.

In his book, *"The 7 Habits of Highly Effective People,"* author Stephen Covey says that thinking about Win-Win isn't about being nice, nor is it a quick-fix technique. It is a character-based code for human interaction and collaboration.

Most of us learn to base our self-worth on comparisons and competition. We think about succeeding in terms of someone else failing -- that is, if I win, you lose; or if you win, I lose. Life becomes a zero sum game.

But Covey says that there is only so much pie to go around. If you get a big piece, there is less for me. It's not fair, and I'm going to make sure you don't get anymore. We all play the game, but how much fun is it really? It is a terrible deal for the loser.

Many people think in terms of either/or: either you're nice or you're tough. Win-win requires that you be both. The Danish attitude is win-win, which requires them to be empathetic, but also have confidence that they will also gain. The system works because Danes agree that this is the best way for their 'samfund' to work.

Much of winning and losing has to do with expectations. As we talked about earlier – with Danish expectations managed correctly, it is possible to make nearly all parties satisfied. Since the Danes have naturally 'managed' expectations win-win is a way of life here and makes for a smooth ride for most.

I stumbled across this famous anecdote called the prisoner's dilemma in which two prisoners must decide whether to confess to a crime.

Neither prisoner knows what the other will do. The best outcome for prisoner A occurs if he/she confesses, while prisoner B keeps quiet. In this case, the prisoner who confesses and implicates the other is rewarded by being set free, and the other (who stayed quiet) receives the maximum sentence, as s/he didn't cooperate with the police, yet they have enough evidence to convict. (This is a win-lose outcome.)

The same goes for prisoner B. But if both prisoners confess (trying to take advantage of their partner), they each serve the maximum sentence (a lose-lose outcome). If neither confesses, they both serve a reduced sentence (a win-win outcome, although the win is not as big as the one they would have received in the win-lose scenario).

This situation occurs fairly often, as win-win outcomes can only be realized when everyone gives in and most of the time it's overlooked since negotiations are often competitive.

Basically the prisoner's dilemma can be summed up in the phrase 'We are all in this together.' And this is closely related to the attitude most Danes have that says that we all choose unselfishly, pay our high taxes and thus, achieve the best possible outcome for everyone.

I believe the Danish system is a transparent prisoner's dilemma. Danes are aware of all the pros and cons like the great personal gains of not paying such high taxes yet they still choose win-win.

People with a win-win attitude see life as a co-operative, egalitarian arena, not a competitive one.

Win-win is a frame of mind, a cultural value and needs a conscience that constantly seeks mutual benefit in all human interactions. Win-win means solutions are mutually advantageous and satisfying.

We both get to eat the pie (or the Danish lagkage), and it tastes pretty darn good!

The Danes Look at the Backside of the Medal

Another thing that help Danes with their happiness is that they are able to talk themselves out of unrealistic dreams and far-fetched material ambitions. Danes have a way of rationalizing their circumstances and are great at seeing the 'glass half full'.

For example, many Danish women say they would *not* dream about having a bigger, more expensive house because cleaning and maintaining it would put a damper on their lifestyle. They would rationalize that a smaller, more cosy house provides them with a better life. Don't get me wrong, I am sure if one of these women were given a huge dream house for free, they would happily clean it but since the 'dream' is out of reach – they don't even dare to fantasize about it.

This makes me think of Aesop's Sour Grapes and a term in psychology called rationalization.

The story goes like this: One hot summer's day a Fox was strolling through an orchard till he came to a bunch of Grapes just ripening on a vine which had been trained over a lofty branch.

"Just the thing to quench my thirst," said he. Drawing back a few paces, he took a run and a jump, and just missed the bunch. Turning round again with a One, Two, Three, he jumped up, but with no greater success.

Again and again he tried after the tempting morsel, but at last had to give it up, and walked away with his nose in the air, saying: "I am sure they are sour."

The problem with Aesop's Sour Grapes is that no one really knows whether the fox was right in his rationalization. Maybe the grapes were really sour, covered in DDT or infested with worms...or simply not really worth the trouble.

A true Danish fox would not even try reaching for them. Why should the fox even bother striving for the unattainable, proverbial grapes?

If the grapes were labeled as 'not interesting'/(LigeGlad) or my favorite term 'whatever' (in Danish – Det lige meget) and a roll of the eyes makes life so much easier and happier, shouldn't we all just pass those damn grapes by.

In general, people deal with — the clashing of conflicting thoughts — by rationalizing one of the thoughts. The idea that the grapes are delicious and sweet conflicts with the knowledge that you can't have them... so you rationalize that it's really not thaaat great and a waste of time and effort.

The entire luxury brand business is built on the concept of high expectations. You need to create envy among your peers in order for the 'item' to have worth. If everyone could afford it, it would lose its luxury status.

What is the point of the envy, why want stuff that is out of reach? The Danes have a saying for this called medallions bagsiden (on the other side of the medal), which pretty much means every prize has a cost....

If we go back to my fox example, let's just say that his ambitious fox friend, Foxy, walked by those grapes and decided he must have them. He builds a ladder out of twigs, which took many weeks and slowly climbed his way up the steep tree. Foxy's work and his sacrifice. (ie. missing the Foxy summer party and a few dates with the cute female foxes that passed by) is the back side of the medal.

Again, my dear Danish Fox would rationalize, the grapes are not sweet enough for that kind of sacrifice!

Most Danes do not want to sacrifice the delicate balance of work and home life for materialistic success. The backside of materialistic success in their eyes is usually hard work, longer hours and sacrifice of family, leisure and quality of life.

Are the Danes better than the rest of us at rationalizing? Are they making delicious, fresh lemonade from the lemons life has given them? Or have they convinced themselves that the lemons indeed taste better than oranges?

This perplexed me for years in Denmark. How can people not have the same cravings for success as me? How could they be happy in their small, cramped, 60's homes and with their tiny cars? Were they secretly stressed, depressed, envious inside or did they simply not value these things.

In Danish, the word for indifference - ligeglad - is used often, especially by children to avoid disappointment.

But unlike the words, 'I don't care' which can be considered rude, being ligeglad is fine. In fact, it is a good coping strategy and way to avoid sadness and disappointment. Ligeglad is a 'happy go lucky' way of saying – I am happy either way!

Funnily enough, if you separate the words into lige glad the words translate into Just Happy.

Trust and Gratitude

During my investigations, I was interviewed on the German/French TV network ARTE about my book and blog. The journalists focused on comparing the most unhappy country in Europe, Hungary, and the most happy, Denmark of course, and wanted to see if they could find out why.

While my interview focused mostly on why I believe the Danes are so happy --- a question off camera came up about trust. For those of us who live here, trust is an accepted virtue.

Denmark is much like the idyllic small town America characterized by the TV show *Mayberry*, where doors are unlocked, real phone numbers are listed in the phone book and corruption is the exception not the rule.

American business columnist Erika Andersen wrote an article in *Forbes* where she mentioned her recent visit to Denmark and her surprising encounter with Danish trust. She and her family were allowed to ride horses on the beach before paying for them, as the stableman trusted that they would reimburse him afterwards.

When you live here – that's nothing!

A quintessential sight in Denmark are babies left to sleep outside in their baby carriages on city sidewalks in the snow and rain while their parents are inside a café drinking café lattes or even shopping.

Young kids here ride their bikes, walk and take the bus and their mothers have few worries about safety. Surveys show that Danes have the highest level of trust in their government, neighbors and even strangers.

I will never forget the day my wallet went missing at the gym and the police refused to believe that it could have been stolen! It must be lost, they assuredly said to me, as they handed me a lost item form, confident that it would show up. (It did.)

According to the 1995-1997 World Value Survey, an amazing 64 percent of Danes believe that 'most people can be trusted' which is three times the world average...

Data suggests that generous social welfare states (those in Nordics) usually have very low levels of corruption and experience a knock-on effect in trust in society, government and this is linked to high levels of happiness and social well-being. In addition, and I think this is very interesting, in countries where trust is high for politicians, police and other public officials, people often assume that strangers and others can be trusted as well.

Researchers have been puzzled by how this happens...which came first? Trusting people creates a welfare state (chicken) or a welfare state creates trusting people (egg)? Experts have not been able to make conclusions about this.

What we do know is that countries with smaller welfare systems tend to be higher in corruption, have lower levels of social trust and lower levels of social well-being, which may explain the unhappiness in Hungary.

Concerning the public sphere, there is a moderate sense of community and civic participation in Hungary. Voter turnout, a measure of public trust in government and of citizens' participation in the political process, was 64% during recent elections; this figure is also lower than the OECD average of 72% and nearly 90% in Denmark. With regards to crime, 4% of people reported falling victim to assault over the previous 12 months.

When asked, 23% of people in Hungary said they were satisfied with their life, much lower than the OECD average of 59%.

The saddest fact was that only 89% of Hungarian people believe that they know someone they could rely on or trust in a time of need.

In addition to trust, Danes are genuinely grateful for their health, home, family, sports and their jobs. People are so grateful for a sunny day, a freshly baked rugbrød or an invitation for a walk in the forest.

There are several ways to express gratitude and say you are thankful: Tusind tak (a thousand thanks). Mange tak (many thanks). Tak for sidst (thanks for our last time), etc.

It's funny, since in Danish we don't even have a word for 'please', but gratitude and thankfulness is very important in everyday language and may provide an insight into why the Danes are so happy.

When you first learn to speak Danish, you realize how important gratitude plays into life and conversation here. Every day after dinner, most kids are expected to give 'thanks' (tak for mad) to their parents for making and providing dinner. Indeed, my daughter, a tweenager, expresses gratitude several times a day, in a very natural and authentic way – to the bus driver, to her teachers, to her classmates.

I have always felt that the word 'thanks' seemed disingenuous and insincere – but since I moved to Denmark and started seeing how it was integrated in nearly all conversations, I began to start using it myself also in English and feeling really good about it. Part of this could be the good karma that is created by filling my mind with thanks for all the wonderful things I have in my life so it opens the door for even more good things to come.

Even little things like collecting the minuscule spring wildflowers called Vintergækken brings joy to Danes. These ever so tiny flowers (which sprout up in the cold, miserable weather) are gathered, dried and sent with a riddle from an anonymous sender – if you guess the sender, you shall thank them with a chocolate egg.

In my diary I try to write a list daily of the small things that I, too, am grateful for — starting from the small things: bit boring...I really liked my breakfast tea, to... wow, I recently got a promotion.

Numerous studies suggest that grateful people are more likely to have higher levels of happiness and lower levels of stress and depression. Grateful people have more positive ways of coping with the difficulties they experience in life, being more likely to seek support from other people, reinterpret and grow from the experience, and spend more time planning how to deal with the problem.

Indeed gratitude has been said to have one of the strongest links with mental health than any other character trait.

Studies also find that gratitude correlates with economic generosity, which works quite well with the large tax state in Denmark. Thankful people are more likely to sacrifice individual gains for communal benefit, supporting the idea that Danes have immense gratitude, have empathy and are generous with their income to help others in the samfund (welfare state).

So what can you do, besides give thanks numerous times a day? Think about things that you are grateful about – a person who has touched your life, write a thank you letter BY HAND, make a gratitude jar where you deposit a post-it note with a thankful message every day or week and then open and read it on a rainy or depressed day.

Mindfulness or Nærvær

During the Danish winter, I experience some bouts of restlessness and crankiness. Normally, I would blame the crap weather and winter for this, but for someone who spends her free time investigating Danish happiness, it is important for me to understand why and try to change it.

While I am aware about why people in Denmark are happy (and I could be too if I changed my attitude!), sometimes it can be difficult to make steps towards a change even if the rewards are great – like eternal happiness and contentment.

The root of my 'so-called' depression is my constant need for improvement, change, gain. While in some ways, these traits make me an excellent manager and a very ambitious employee, it can also lead me to unhappiness, despair and a feeling of powerlessness when things do not move in my favor. As my Danish coach clearly pointed out, my need for constant approval makes me an insatiable hungry dog. Each time I get a bone I quickly devour it and beg for more.

She suggested that I start practicing mindfulness or, in Danish, 'Nærvær.

When I started looking into it, mindfulness is already readily present in Danish culture, although the concept is based in Buddhist philosophy. Mindfulness is about the present, living in the present and enjoying and experiencing the moment like right now. It is about concentrating your thoughts about the mundane part of your day – eating an apple, drinking tea or walking to the bus.

Danish design may also play a part. For many years, I never understood why Danes would covet a designer salt shaker. This Christmas, I received a Georg Jensen salt shaker as a present. It is a beautiful piece of art, stainless steel, it sits beautifully on the table and it sits well in your hands.

But each time I use it, I don't necessarily pay attention to the experience. Should it be an experience to shake salt on your food?

Since the everyday mindfulness did not appeal to me (drink tea without sugar?, PLEAAASE), I decided to do something kind of crazy- like extreme mindfulness. I tried Nordic winter bathing. Winter bathing is really popular here (The Charlottenlund winter bathers club is notorious for its 5 year long waiting list) and according to some devout practitioners, it is a way of truly healthy mindful living.

One of my Danish girlfriends, Ms. WB is a daily dip winter bather – she goes out in rain, shine, hail, sleet into the ocean and says it is the most amazing and invigorating experience ever.

Me: 'I'm thinking about winter bathing in order to find comfort in 'my discomfort.'

WB: 'Yes, do it- you will love it, Plunging into the water is like being re-born,' she says. 'You get addicted to the feelings, the rush and emotion of just you and the ocean. Blood rushes through your veins, your body is pumped with adrenaline and you feel so warm.

Me: 'Wow, can't believe such a high is just around the corner from me. I don't even need to visit Pusher Street in Christiania'

WB: But the best part is afterwards, you feel so warm inside, it's like your internal heat volcano erupts.'

What a sell, (total high, re-birth and internal volcanos – so cool!) I was ready to go, I thought. Maybe I should put myself on the winter bather's waiting list, since I will be hooked on winter bathing after this, I thought to myself.

Thomas Jefferson also believed in the potential health benefits of winter bathing; every morning he began each day by soaking his feet in ice water. Jefferson also slept sitting up, so maybe I should not use him as a good example.

Anyway, one weekend, in the subzero cold, I threw myself into the ocean - naked. Literally, for like two seconds. (For some reason, you need to be nude in order to not get sick from 'wet clothes.')

Within moments I started to think of myself as a practitioner of mindless 'ness' when suddenly my foot went completely numb and started throbbing like crazy. God, was this my insane way to find happiness and contentment... what was I doing? I really started to panic, as I froze, still in the water, paralyzed.

I made my way to the edge of the water to my bathrobe, crawled feverishly to my car, where I eventually sat with the heat on full blast. I began to start to really appreciate everything around me...anything was better than the freezing icy water....Jesus, sitting in the car was a dream.

I am not sure whether I have the guts to continue winter bathing, albeit the amazing effects of it.

That said, you really appreciate the basics in life (like clothes), after nearly dying of hypothermia in the dark ocean plus I did feel eerily warm inside.

After this dreadful experience, I have started on a new regime of Danish 'winter' bathing. Well, actually it is summer bathing in cold Danish waters (16 degrees) but I am working towards the winter – one degree at a time. I think this activity actually gives me some feelings of flow – a state of joy, total involvement, exhilaration and just for a few moments my problems seem to melt away.

Let's go back to our Happiness Recipe: the most fascinating part of this equation was the percentage (weights) breakdown of the different parts. They are:

50% Your happiness DNA- **Self**
10% Conditions of living- **Life**
40% Voluntary actions or choices you make daily- **Activities**

In an attempt to be happier **H**, most people focus the majority of their attention on changing their conditions of living, like me, by trying to make more money, live a luxury lifestyle or move to Hawaii. But as the equation shows, that only makes up 10%.

So just goes to show, so much of personal happiness could be gained with the 'right' choices.

It was here that all the lessons of the past few years of investigation began to unfold before me.

A Piece of Love and Happiness

My last chapter is actually one of the most important keys to happiness which is love, relationships and family. As you know, I started this book with my broken life story and I promise that this has a happy ending. ☺

I spent 2 years searching, thinking and dreaming about the meaning of Danish happiness. It was a struggle because at first, I must admit, Danes are not an easy group to comprehend. But for me admittedly as a 'New' Dane, the culture was beginning to grow on me, changing my thinking, so it became more difficult to decipher Danish perspectives from my own.

In Denmark, we have a beautiful concept called Livskunst, it means the art of living and caring for others. At first I thought it was a boho concept but now it really symbolizes my life today.

Gosh, where do I start? For a former Hindu American Princess, I did one of the most outrageous and crazy things possible...I fell in love with a guy with a huge debt, no money and 3 kids. In my 'old glory' days, a guy with no money was a useless twat and would never, ever be able to talk to me and most certainly not date me.

Most of my American friends dreamt of being swept off their feet by a good natured, personable millionaire in order to escape the humdrum and toil of earning a living. I thought my dream life was overflowing with fast cars, fine dining, fancy villas and fame and fortune. Some of these women, in fact, are still looking for ways to find a rich man to marry.

I read once that as primates, women were drawn to men who were powerful, agile, able to provide and protect. In today's world this amounts to money, career and success and in the past attracted the most number of women. Thus it is an instinct nurtured over thousands of years.

As Marilyn Monroe remarked in her movie, 'Gentlemen prefer Blondes', 'Don't you know that a man being rich is like a woman being pretty?'

But when I looked at my Danish female friends they fell for different things in a man: his personality, his manners, his character, his education and family or inevitably, his body. I must admit it was inspiring.

Actually many of my divorced female friends were actually dating younger men who were the 'opposite' of their older, more established ex-husbands.

My 2 past husbands were wealthy, successful men yet those relationships failed. I felt that I had a big hand in this as the importance I attached to money destroyed my happiness and satisfaction in those relationships.

Part of my attraction to men in the past was that they could provide me with the 'luxury lifestyle' I was accustomed to having. But by living in Denmark, that lifestyle no longer made sense anymore.

I needed a partner for my new lifestyle and this tall, handsome, blonde, blue-eyed creature helped show me the way to find it, Mr. J.

I am immensely happy and 6 years afterwards, I still feel that he fulfills the romantic dream of my life. My loving relationship has intense passion but it is also filled companionship, friendship and adventure. Because I stopped focusing on material things I wanted – I automatically became less critical and stopped blaming others for my unhappiness. I also started being more grateful and appreciative for what I did have – like, Mr. J did not have a lot of money – but he does have a great job and together we were actually a very strong couple.

In addition I started changing the way I dealt with negativity or relationship problems with an AAA: an Apology, Affection, and a promise of Action. You say you're sorry for what you've said or done to hurt or disappoint your partner. You immediately offer a hug, a kiss—some meaningful gesture of warmth. You pledge to do something that matters to your partner ('From now on, I will...'). And, of course, you stick to that.

This whole AAA thing can take two minutes, but in that time you've healed the past, built a bridge to the present, and created hope for your future.

Danish families are the crux of society in Denmark and they come in all shapes and sizes – in a classroom it is typical to see single parents, re-married parents and even legally married gay couples with their adopted child.

My new family with new husband and 50 percent daughter means I am now on my third marriage – (Elizabeth Taylor, you got competition!) And while I am much happier now there are times it can be a struggle to always see things in the 'Danish light.'

For example, I am not always that good about making limoncello with the life lemons I am handed. And I still sometimes get frustrated with 'not having enough' and wanting more stuff than I have or can afford.

The other day, I bought an amazing iPad. It has changed my life -- it so fantastic to have the information of the world at a moment's notice at my fingertips. I love it.

Unfortunately I also felt that I 'needed' a Gucci iPad cover as well. And my new Danish husband didn't agree. We had a major argument outside the Gucci store, where I became angry about his insensitive comments. He knows I was a HAP and once in awhile I just need a bit of luxury.

After I bought the cover he chided, 'Well your useless designer cover is more expensive than the iPad.' He had a point as six months later, I found the iPad cover, all dusty, under the bed -unused.

But besides the few setbacks, I have cut back on the shoe obsession. I have sold some of my shoes on DBA (the Danish ebay) and have even bought myself a pair of sensible Danish leather clogs. Yes, I wear them gladly with jeans and it means now I can run for the bus without landing headfirst on the pavement.

Mr J is literally a walking dream. And what I love about our relationship is that we are equals (we split our household economy in half and I contribute to everything) and this I believe is one of the reasons that both men and women are happy and satisfied here.

In addition to splitting stuff financially, we also divide all household duties. Men in Denmark are in touch with their feminine side. This means, early on, they are taught cooking, sewing, cleaning and even child rearing. It is more and more common to see fathers staying home with the kids and we even have fathers' playgroups and other support groups for these *house husbands*.

The Danish system allows both parents to share the maternity/paternity leave and many men do their part and stay home with the newborns.

The Mr.J , although an Executive Vice President of a mid-sized company, was also great at ironing and cleaning windows. In the early days, I sweetly offered to iron his wrinkly shirt and started gently jabbing it with the iron.

'Hey, hey, I don't want you to hurt yourself,' he said, as he quickly grabbed his tailored Hugo Boss Egyptian cotton shirt off the ironing board. 'You have never ironed a shirt before, have you?,' he asked with a crooked smile.

My Mr J, well let's just say he is a master at washing the floors. Most Scandinavian homes have these white washed floors that can end up pretty streaky once I have washed them. But the floors look polished, pearl-like when he is finished.

On the other hand, I do most of the grocery shopping and we usually make a simple dinner together and something more fancy with friends in the weekends.

It is a peaceful and harmonious life. Admittedly, sometimes a bit boring...

A question I am always asked is – are you a happy Dane? I would say yes and no.

I think the Danish mentality of lowered expectations is too fundamentally against my values as an American. For me, it is about setting realistic goals, instead of lowered goals and in that way, finding my own balance between both success and happiness and melding both cultures.

My DH and I have goals and ambitions for our life together. We save towards our retirement, we renovate and improve our home (ourselves) and yes, we both drive BMWs because they are nice to drive, but are also a kind of a luxury.

My project has been a personal journey for myself with the help of the Jante law.

The reflections I have made through my online blog, numerous interviews and discussions has led me to live a more virtuous life, and I see that through the way other people respond to me and my husband.

Our friends, families, co-workers and neighbors trust and rely on us. They come to us for guidance and help, and their kids want to be around us because we inspire them to think in new and different ways, and yet still embrace Danish culture with hygge, mindfulness, exercise, engagement with nature and family values.

Making the right choices, valuing family, friends and community and yet still striving for excellence in our work and in all we do is our mantra. Can life be lived any better?

[i] (Biswas-Diener, Vittersø, & Diener, 2010)
[ii] (Veenhoven, 2009)
[iii] (Biswas-Diener et al., 2010)
[iv] Biswas-Diener et al., 2010).
[v] Dam, Jokobsen, & Mellerup, 1998).tiful nature (Argyle, 2001).

[vi] (Csikszentmihalyi and Wong 1991).

5537090R00126

Made in the USA
San Bernardino, CA
10 November 2013